interchange

English for international communication

Jack C. Richards

with Jonathan Hull
and Susan Proctor

3

Student's Book

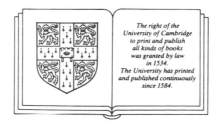

The right of the
University of Cambridge
to print and publish
all kinds of books
was granted by law
in 1534.
The University has printed
and published continuously
since 1584.

Cambridge University Press

Cambridge • New York • Port Chester • Melbourne • Sydney

Published by the Press Syndicate of the University of Cambridge
The Pitt Building, Trumpington Street, Cambridge CB2 1RP
40 West 20th Street, New York, NY 10011, USA
10 Stamford Road, Oakleigh, Melbourne 3166, Australia

© Cambridge University Press 1991

First published 1991

Printed in the United States of America

Library of Congress Cataloging-in-Publication Data
Richards, Jack C.
Interchange : English for international communication : student's
book 3 / Jack C. Richards with Jonathan Hull and Susan Proctor;
[illustrators, Mark Kaufman . . . et al.].
p. cm.
ISBN 0-521-37684-X (paperback). – ISBN 0-521-37685-8 (teacher's
manual). – ISBN 0-521-37686-6 (workbook). – ISBN 0-521-37536-3
(class cassette). – ISBN 0-521-37537-1 (student cassette)
1. English language – Textbooks for foreign speakers.   I. Hull,
Jonathan.   II. Proctor, Susan.   III. Title.
[PE1128.R457   1991]
428.2'4 – dc20   91-9509
                                                              CIP

British Library Cataloguing in Publication Data
Richards, J. C. (Jack Croft)
Interchange : English for international communication.
1. English language
I. Title   II. Hull, Jonathan   III. Proctor, Susan
428
ISBN 0-521-37684-X

ISBN 0 521 37684 X Student's Book Three
ISBN 0 521 37685 8 Teacher's Manual Three
ISBN 0 521 37686 6 Workbook Three
ISBN 0 521 37536 3 Class Cassette Set Three
ISBN 0 521 37537 1 Student Cassette Three

Book design: Peter Ducker
Layout and design services: McNally Graphic Design

Illustrators:
Mark Kaufman
Joseph Sellars
Bill Thomson
Sam Viviano

Contents

Plan of Book 3

	Topics	Functions	Grammar/Pronunciation
UNIT 1	**Topics** Personal qualities; relationships	**Functions** Describing personalities; describing childhood and school days	**Grammar** Clauses with *who, that, when;* adverbial clauses of time **Pronunciation** Emphatic stress
UNIT 2	**Topics** Jobs; careers; education; skills	**Functions** Describing and comparing jobs; describing skills and abilities	**Grammar** Comparisons; adverbs of degree and adjectives **Pronunciation** Sentence stress
UNIT 3	**Topics** Cities and places; climate	**Functions** Describing cities and places; giving a class talk	**Grammar** Order of adjectives, quantifiers with countable and uncountable nouns **Pronunciation** Reduced forms of *there are/there is*

Review of Units 1–3

	Topics	Functions	Grammar/Pronunciation
UNIT 4	**Topics** The media; news stories; past events; dreams	**Functions** Describing past events; narrating a story; describing a dream	**Grammar** Questions with past tense; past tense and past continuous **Pronunciation** Reduced and blended forms in Wh-questions
UNIT 5	**Topics** Requests; messages	**Functions** Making requests; accepting/declining requests; leaving messages	**Grammar** Requests with modals and *if*-clauses; indirect requests **Pronunciation** Blended consonants
UNIT 6	**Topics** Schools; marriage; work; preferences	**Functions** Asking about preferences; describing differences and similarities	**Grammar** *Would rather* and *prefer;* quantifiers **Pronunciation** Intonation in questions of choice

Review of Units 4–6

	Topics	Functions	Grammar/Pronunciation
UNIT 7	**Topics** Cities and places; tourism; customs; advice	**Functions** Describing cities and places; talking about customs; giving advice	**Grammar** Adverbials of purpose and reason; clauses with *when* and *if* **Pronunciation** Consonant clusters with /s/
UNIT 8	**Topics** Shopping; services; recommendations	**Functions** Asking where to get something done; asking for recommendations	**Grammar** *Get* and *have* + participle; nouns with infinitives; clauses with *because* **Pronunciation** Consonant contrast with /s/ and /ʃ/

Topics	Functions	Grammar/Pronunciaton
UNIT 9	**Topics** History; biography; the future	**Functions** Talking about historical events; talking about the future	**Grammar** Prepositions and adverbs; future with *will, going to*, future continuous, future perfect **Pronunciation** Syllable stress

Review of Units 7–9

UNIT 10	**Topics** Homes; household appliances; complaints	**Functions** Describing homes and neighborhoods; renting an apartment; describing problems; making complaints; offering to fix something	**Grammar** Conjunctions, adverbs, and prepositions **Pronunciation** Contrastive stress
UNIT 11	**Topics** Social and environmental issues; hypothetical situations	**Functions** Giving opinions; describing hypothetical situations	**Grammar** *If*-clauses and modals; phrases with gerunds **Pronunciation** Plural *s*
UNIT 12	**Topics** Gadgets and appliances; inventions; processes	**Functions** Describing how something works; describing what something is used for; describing a process	**Grammar** Relative clauses; the passive **Pronunciation** Stress in compound nouns

Review of Units 10–12

UNIT 13	**Topics** Mysteries; unexplained events; predicaments	**Functions** Giving explanations; describing hypothetical events	**Grammar** Modals and past modals **Pronunciation** Reduced forms in past modals
UNIT 14	**Topics** Success; advertising	**Functions** Giving reasons; describing qualities for success; comparing ads	**Grammar** Sentences with *if*-clauses and infinitives **Pronunciation** Reduced forms
UNIT 15	**Topics** Opinions; problems; controversial issues	**Functions** Giving and acknowledging opinions; asking for and giving reasons; agreeing and disagreeing; ending a discussion	**Grammar** Tag questions and responses **Pronunciation** Intonation in tag questions

Review of Units 13–15

Interchange Activities

Listening	Writing/Reading	Interchange Activity	
Listening Listening to biographical information; listening to a description	**Writing** Writing a biography **Reading** World history; who really discovered America?	**Interchange** History quiz	UNIT **9**
		Review of Units 7–9	
Listening Listening to information on housing; listening to complaints	**Writing** Writing a letter of complaint **Reading** Home truths; marking personal territory	**Interchange** Customer complaints	UNIT **10**
Listening Listening to opinions and suggestions	**Writing** Writing about opinions **Reading** Pollution; garbage disposal/recycling	**Interchange** Talking about predicaments	UNIT **11**
Listening Listening to descriptions; listening for a process	**Writing** Writing about how something is made **Reading** Useless facts; advertisements	**Interchange** Describing and identifying items	UNIT **12**
		Review of Units 10–12	
Listening Listening to possibilities; choosing the best suggestion	**Writing** Writing about an awkward situation **Reading** Unsolved mysteries; the case of the missing pilot	**Interchange** Survival quiz	UNIT **13**
Listening Listening to an interview; listening to a radio commercial	**Writing** Writing about how to be successful **Reading** Success stories; new ideas in advertising	**Interchange** Creating a commercial	UNIT **14**
Listening Listening to opinions and reasons	**Writing** Writing about opinions **Reading** Unusual laws; animal rights	**Interchange** Class debate	UNIT **15**
		Review of Units 13–15	
		Interchange Activities	

Acknowledgments

Text Credits

7 Reprinted by permission of Sterling Lord Literistics, Inc. Copyright © 1989 by John Deadline Enterprises, Inc.
13 From NEWSWEEK, 25 April 1988, © 1988, Newsweek, Inc. All rights reserved. Reprinted by permission.
14 *(Snapshot)* Copyright © 1990 by the New York Times Company. Reprinted by permission.
27 From *The National Examiner,* 18 July 1989. Reprinted by permission.
39 From Joseph Tobin, David Wu, and Dana Davidson, "How Three Key Countries Shape Their Children," *World Monitor,* April 1989. Reprinted by permission.
67 Text and chart from *Eye to Eye* by Dr. Peter Marsh. Copyright © 1988 by Andromeda Osford, Ltd. Reprinted by permission of HarperCollins Publishers.
87 Copyright 1989 by *Omni Magazine* and reprinted with the permission of Omni Publications International, Ltd.
93 Text and illustrations taken from *283 Useful Ideas from Japan* by Leonard Koren © 1989 Chronicle Books.

Illustrators

Mark Kaufman   23, 40, 62, 66 *(both)*, 78 *(bottom)*, 94
Joseph Sellars   75, 78 *(top)*, 101, 114 *(all)*, 116 *(all)*
Bill Thomson   2, 5, 8, 13, 20, 25, 33, 41, 44, 58, 64, 72, 74, 81 *(top)*, 85 *(bottom)*, 95, 98
Sam Viviano   3, 26, 29, 32, 37, 38, 50, 65, 68, 69, 81 *(bottom)*, 85 *(top)*, 90, 96, 100, 105, 106, 107, 113
Snapshots by Phil Scheuer

Photographic Credits

The authors and publishers are grateful for permission to reproduce the following photographs.

4   Dario Perla/International Stock Photography
6   Tom Rosenthal/SuperStock
7   Gwendolen Cates
9   *(top)* Camérique/H. Armstrong Roberts; *(bottom)* Will Mosgrove/Courtesy Apple Computer
10   *(left)* © 1984 Gabe Palmer/The Stock Market; *(right)* © David Greenfield
11   Fredric Petters
12   *(left)* © Mitchell Funk/The Image Bank; *(right)* © 1986 Jane Art Ltd./The Image Bank
14   Ralph Krubner/H. Armstrong Roberts
15   © Luis Castañeda/The Image Bank
16   *(top, left to right)* Alan Bolesta/Index Stock International; H. Armstrong Roberts; National Center for Atmospheric Research/National Science Foundation; *(bottom)* FPG International
17   *(top)* Frank Wood/SuperStock; *(bottom)* Larry Lee/H. Armstrong Roberts
18   *(top)* W. Bertsch/H. Armstrong Roberts; *(bottom)* G. Roessler/H. Armstrong Roberts
19   *(top right)* Index Stock International; *(bottom left, both)* The Photo Library, Sydney
20   D. Degnan/H. Armstrong Roberts
21   San Francisco Convention and Visitors Bureau photo by Kerrick James

23   © 1991 CAPITAL CITIES/ABC, INC. (Steve Fenn)
34   © 1990 Mug Shots/The Stock Market
35   *(from top to bottom)* © H. Scott Heist 1990 for Northampton Community College; Steve Weinrebe/Stock Boston; E. Alan McGee/FPG International
36   *(from left to right)* Roy King/SuperStock; SuperStock; © James Davis/International Stock Photography
37   Sally and Richard Greenhill
39   *(both)* Richard H. Hinze, Ed.D.
42   *(top)* John Moss/Photo Researchers; *(bottom)* Iara Venazi/Kino Fotoarquivo
43   *(top)* Robert Phillips/The Image Bank; *(bottom)* National Park Service/R. M. Butterfield
44   *(top)* Cosmo Condina/Index Stock International; *(bottom)* courtesy of Kumiko Sekioka
45   Japan National Tourist Organization
46   K. Scholz/H. Armstrong Roberts
47   *(left)* © Bill Lyons, Amman, Jordan; *(right)* Adamsmith/Westlight/H. Armstrong Roberts
48   Stephen Turk
50   *(left)* SuperStock; *(right)* S. Vidler/SuperStock
51   © 1986 Ron Calamia/New Orleans Tourist and Convention Commission
52   *(top)* M. Thonig/H. Armstrong Roberts; *(bottom, both)* San Antonio Convention and Visitor's Bureau
53   *(clockwise from top left)* courtesy of PARCO, Tokyo, Japan; J. Schuyler/Stock Boston; H. Armstrong Roberts; courtesy of Savoy Hotel, London
54   Jacques Witt/SIPA
55   The Bettmann Archive
56   *(from top to bottom)* Jay Freis/The Image Bank; National Aeronautics and Space Administration; from the collection of David Loehr
57   *(top)* The Bettmann Archive; *(bottom)* Oshihara/SIPA
59   *(top)* Historical Picture Service/FPG International; *(bottom)* The Bettmann Archive
60   © 1988 Kevin Forest/The Image Bank
61   *(top)* ZEFA/H. Armstrong Roberts; *(bottom)* Steve Vidler/SuperStock
63   G. Glod/SuperStock
64   *(top)* Wallace Garrison/Index Stock International; *(bottom)* SuperStock
71   *(left)* SuperStock; *(right)* R. Allyn Lee/SuperStock
73   *(both)* Courtesy of the Tokyo Metropolitan Government and the Machida Recycling Center
76   *(clockwise from top right)* Copyright © The Sharper Image; courtesy of Black and Decker; courtesy of Hammacher Schlemmer, 1-800-543-3366
77   Catherine Karnow
79   *(SwimEx minipool)* Courtesy of SwimEx Systems, Inc.; *(VOICE computer Explorer)* courtesy of Voice Computer Corp.; *(Cafe San)* courtesy of SANYO Consumer Electronics; *(Blood Pressure Monitor and Denonet Singing System)* courtesy of The Sharper Image
80   Joseph Nettis/Stock Boston
82   Smithsonian Institution Photo No. 88-19752
83   *(left)* J. Chimbidis/FPG International; *(right)* The Stock Market
84   SuperStock
87   © Tim White

90 *(top)* SuperStock; *(bottom)* © 1990 Keith Kent
91/134 Courtesy of SANYO
92 *(from left to right)*/**133** Courtesy of Young &
Rubicam Advertising, San Francisco, Art Direction:
Melinda W. Mettler, Copywriting Gayle Keck,
Photography: Dennis Bettencourt; courtesy of Skin Cancer
Foundation; courtesy of Northwest Airlines
96 George de Steinheil
97 Sally and Richard Greenhill
99 © J. Barry O'Rourke
100 *(left)* SuperStock; *(right)* Buddy Jenssen/Index
Stock International
101 Sandra J. Graham
104 *(top)* J. Barnell/SuperStock; *(bottom)* Dave Forbert/
SuperStock

109 *(both)* © H. Scott Heist 1990 for Northampton
Community College
110 *(clockwise from top)* Peter Miller/The Image Bank;
French Government Tourist Office; © 1990 Welzenbach/
The Stock Market; French Government Tourist Office
111 *(top)* Courtesy of Radio Shack, A Division of Tandy
Corporation; *(bottom)* Zenith Electronics Corporation
112 *(top)* This is a photograph of a model 087 W hair
dryer developed by Conair Corporation, Stamford,
Connecticut, U.S.A., which introduced the first pistol grip
hair dryer in the U.S.A.; *(bottom)* courtesy of Nikon
115 National Aeronautics and Space Administration
117 *(from top to bottom)* courtesy of Dahon California
Inc.; courtesy of Zenith Data Systems; courtesy of Nike,
Inc.

Authors' Acknowledgments

A great number of people assisted us in writing **Interchange.** We owe particular
thanks to the following:

Our **reviewers,** who gave helpful comments on preliminary versions of the
course:

Fred E. Anderson, Jeffrey Bright, Steven Brown, Marc Helgesen, Thomas
Mandeville, Suzanne Robertshaw, Charles Sandy, and Rita Wong.

The **students** and **teachers** in the following schools and institutes who pilot
tested components of **Interchange;** their valuable comments and suggestions
helped shape the content of the entire course:

Adult ESL Administrative Resource Centre, Toronto Board of Education,
Toronto, Canada; **Adult Learning Skills Program, Truman College,** Chicago,
Illinois, U.S.A.; **Alianza Cultural Uruguay-Estados Unidos de America,**
Montevideo, Uruguay; **American Language Center,** Casablanca, Morocco;
American Language Center, University of California at Los Angeles, U.S.A.;
American Language Institute, American College in Paris, France; **American
Language Institute, New York University,** New York, U.S.A.; **American
Language Program, American Center,** Paris, France; **Associação Alumni,** São
Paulo, Brazil; **Centre de Récherches et d'Applications Pédagogiques en
Langues,** Nancy, France; **Centro Boliviano Americano,** La Paz, Bolivia; **D. B.
Hood Community School,** Toronto, Canada; **Eastdale Collegiate,** Toronto,
Canada; **Eurocentres,** Alexandria, Virginia, U.S.A.; **International English
Service,** Okayama, Japan; **Instituto Cultural Mexicano-Norteamericano de
Jalisco,** Guadalajara, Mexico; **Intensive English Program, University of
Central Florida,** Orlando, Florida, U.S.A.; **Impact Institute,** Santiago, Chile;
Interac, Tokyo, Japan; **La Guardia Community College,** New York, U.S.A.;
International House, Budapest, Hungary; **Kanda Gaigo Gakuin,** Tokyo, Japan;
Kyoto YMCA English Conversation School, Kyoto, Japan; **Loma Vista Adult
Center, Mt. Diablo Adult Education,** Concord, California, U.S.A.; **Migros-
Klub-Schule,** Bern, Switzerland; **Mohawk College, English Language Studies,**
Hamilton, Ontario, Canada; **New Day School,** Sendai, Japan; **Nihonbashi
Women's Junior College,** Chiba, Japan; **Nunoike Language School,** Nagoya,
Japan; **Ontario Welcome House,** Toronto, Canada; **Overseas Training Center,**
Osaka, Japan; **Panterra American School,** Fontanelle, Italy; **Seneca College,**
Toronto, Canada; **Sheridan College,** Mississauga, Ontario, Canada; **Tokyo
Foreign Language College,** Tokyo, Japan; and **University of Pittsburgh
English Language Institute,** Tokyo, Japan.

And our **editors** and **advisors** at Cambridge University Press, who guided us
through the complex process of writing classroom materials:

Suzette André, Peter Donovan, Adrian du Plessis, Sandra Graham, Colin Hayes,
Steven Maginn, Ellen Shaw, and Marjan van Schaik.

Introduction

Interchange is a three-level course in English as a second or foreign language for young adults and adults. The course covers the skills of listening, speaking, reading, and writing, with particular emphasis on listening and speaking. The primary goal of the course is to teach communicative competence – that is, the ability to communicate in English according to the situation, purpose, and roles of the participants. *Interchange* reflects the fact that English is the world's major language of international communication and is not limited to any one country, region, or culture. Level Three takes students from intermediate to high intermediate level.

Level Three builds on and extends the foundations for accurate and fluent communication established in Levels One and Two. Following a similar approach and methodology, Level Three extends the learners' grammatical, lexical, and functional skills, enabling them to consolidate and develop their communicative competence in English through the use of a wide variety of stimulating and challenging activities. A range of higher-level comprehension skills is also developed. Listening activities involve listening to narratives, commercials, discussions, and interviews, some taken from authentic sources such as radio broadcasts. Reading activities are derived from authentic sources and often reflect cross-cultural themes, exploring life-styles and values in different countries. Throughout Level Three, learners are given ample opportunity for personal expression in the form of pair work, group work, and discussion.

COURSE LENGTH

Interchange is a self-contained course covering all four language skills. Each level covers between 60 and 90 hours of class instruction time. Depending on how the book is used, however, more or less time may be utilized. The Teacher's Manual gives detailed suggestions for optional activities to extend each unit. Where less time is available, the course can be taught in approximately 60 hours by reducing the amount of time spent on Interchange Activities, reading, writing, optional activities, and the Workbook.

COURSE COMPONENTS

Student's Book   The Student's Book contains fifteen units, with a review unit after every three units. There are five review units in all. Following Unit 15 is a set of communication activities called Interchange Activities, one for each unit of the book. Unit Summaries, at the end of the Student's Book, contain lists of the key vocabulary and expressions used in each unit as well as grammar summaries.

Teacher's Manual   A separate Teacher's Manual contains detailed suggestions on how to teach the course, lesson-by-lesson notes, an extensive set of optional follow-up activities, complete answer keys to the Student's Book and Workbook exercises, tests for use in class and test answer keys, and transcripts of those listening activities not printed in the Student's Book and in the five tests. The tests can be photocopied and distributed to students after each review unit is completed.

Workbook   The Workbook contains stimulating and varied exercises that provide additional practice on the teaching points presented in the Student's Book. A variety of exercise types is used to develop students' skills in grammar, reading, writing, spelling, vocabulary, and pronunciation. The Workbook can be used both for classwork and for homework.

Class Cassettes   A set of two cassettes for class use accompanies the Student's Book. The cassettes contain recordings of the conversations, grammar focus summaries, pronunciation exercises, and listening activities, as well as recordings of the listening exercises used in the tests. A variety of native-speaker voices and accents is used, as well as some non-native speakers of English. Exercises that are recorded on the cassettes are indicated with the symbol ▭.

Student Cassette   A cassette is also available for students to use for self-study. The Student Cassette contains selected recordings of conversations, grammar, and pronunciation exercises from the Student's Book.

APPROACH AND METHODOLOGY

Interchange teaches students to use English for everyday situations and purposes related to work, school, social life, and leisure. The underlying philosophy of the course is that learning a second language is more rewarding, meaningful, and effective when the language is used for authentic communication. Information-sharing activities provide a maximum amount of student-generated communication. Throughout *Interchange,* students have the opportunity to personalize the language they learn and make use of their own life experiences and world knowledge.

The course has the following key features:

Integrated Syllabus *Interchange* has an integrated, multi-skills syllabus that links grammar and communicative functions. The course recognizes grammar as an essential component of second language proficiency. However, it presents grammar communicatively, with controlled accuracy-based activities leading to fluency-based communicative practice. The syllabus also contains the four skills of listening, speaking, reading, and writing, as well as pronunciation and vocabulary.

Adult and International Content *Interchange* deals with contemporary topics that are of high interest and relevance to both students and teachers. Each unit includes real-world information on a variety of topics.

Enjoyable and Useful Learning Activities A wide variety of interesting and enjoyable activities forms the basis for each unit. The course makes extensive use of pair work, small group activities, role plays, and information-sharing activities. Practice exercises allow for a maximum amount of individual student practice and enable learners to personalize and apply the language they learn. Throughout the course, natural and useful language is presented that can be used in real-life situations.

WHAT EACH UNIT CONTAINS

Each unit in *Interchange* contains the following kinds of exercises:

Snapshot The Snapshots contain interesting and often amusing information about the world. They introduce the topic of the unit and extend students' vocabulary. In Level Three, Snapshot exercises involve class discussion tasks that serve to prepare the students for activities that will be introduced elsewhere in the unit.

Conversation The Conversations introduce the new grammar of each unit in a communicative context and also present functions and conversational expressions. They often lead into follow-up listening and discussion tasks or role play activities that allow the learners to personalize the content of the conversations.

Pronunciation These exercises focus on important features of spoken English, including stress, rhythm, intonation, reductions, and sound contrasts.

Grammar Focus The new grammar of each unit is presented in color panels and is followed by practice activities that move from controlled to freer practice. These activities always give students a chance to use the grammar they have learned for real communication.

Listening The listening activities develop a wide variety of listening skills, including listening for gist, listening for details, and inferring meaning from context. In Level Three, students listen to extended discourse, such as monologs, narratives, and interviews. These exercises often require completing an authentic task while listening, such as taking telephone messages, note taking, and summarizing. The recordings on the Class Cassettes contain both scripted and unscripted conversations with natural pauses, hesitations, and interruptions that occur in real speech.

Word Power The Word Power activities develop students' vocabulary through a variety of interesting tasks, such as word maps.

Writing The writing exercises include practical writing tasks that extend and reinforce the teaching points in the unit and help develop students' composition skills. The Teacher's Manual shows how to use these exercises to focus on the process of writing.

Reading The reading passages develop a variety of reading skills, including guessing words from context, skimming, scanning, and making inferences. Various text types adapted from authentic sources are used.

Interchange Activities The Interchange Activities are pair work and group work tasks, information-sharing tasks, and role plays that encourage real communication. These exercises are a central part of the course and allow students to extend and personalize what they have learned in each unit.

From the Authors

We hope that you will like using *Interchange* and find it useful, interesting, and fun. Our goal has been to provide teachers and students with activities that make the English class a time to look forward to and, at the same time, provide students with the skills they need to use English outside the classroom. Please let us know how you enjoyed it, and good luck!

Jack C. Richards
Jonathan Hull
Susan Proctor

1 That's what friends are for

1 CONVERSATION 📼

1 Listen.

Dave: Hello?
Jim: Hi. My name's Jim Brady. I'm calling about the ad for a roommate.
Dave: Oh, yes.
Jim: Are you still looking for someone?
Dave: Yes, we are.
Jim: Oh, good. I'm really interested.
Dave: Well, there are four of us, and it's a fairly small house, so we want someone who's easy to get along with.
Jim: Well, I'm pretty easygoing.
Dave: Great! Can I ask you a few questions?

2 Think of three questions Dave might ask Jim. Then listen to the rest of the conversation. What questions did Dave ask?

3 Do you think Jim is reliable? Do you think he will move in?

4 *Role play* Close your books and have a conversation like the one between Dave and Jim. Use your own questions and your own information.

2 WORD POWER: Adjectives

1 *Pair work* Match each word with a definition. Then mark if each word has a positive (+) or negative (−) meaning.

a) easygoing
b) emotional
c) generous
d) independent
e) moody
f) patient
g) proud
h) sociable
i) unreliable

.... people who don't do what they say they will
.... a person who doesn't often ask for other people's help or advice
.... a person who waits calmly for things and doesn't worry if things are not on time
.... someone who likes giving things to other people
.... a person who doesn't usually worry or get angry
.... someone who is often gloomy or depressed
.... a person who enjoys being with other people
.... people who have a high opinion of their own importance
.... people who show their feelings easily

Now give definitions for these words: **ambitious, punctual, selfish.**

2

2 *Group work*   What qualities should a friend have? Think of five adjectives.

3 Now listen to the conversation in Exercise 1 again and choose an adjective to describe Jim.

3 GRAMMAR FOCUS: Clauses with *who, that, when*

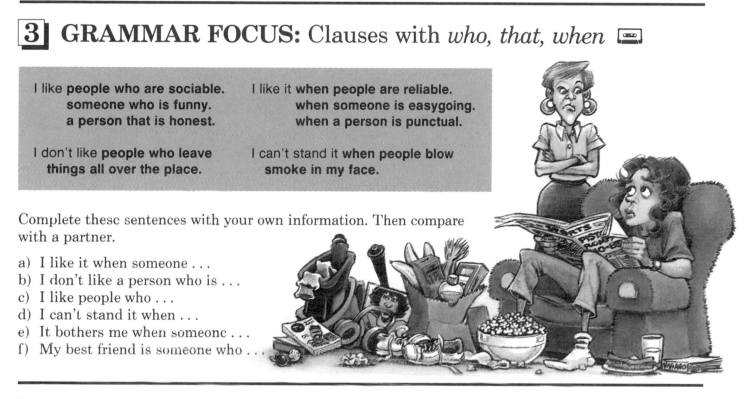

> I like **people who are sociable.**
>   **someone who is funny.**
>   **a person that is honest.**
>
> I don't like **people who leave things all over the place.**

> I like it **when people are reliable.**
>   **when someone is easygoing.**
>   **when a person is punctual.**
>
> I can't stand it **when people blow smoke in my face.**

Complete these sentences with your own information. Then compare with a partner.

a) I like it when someone . . .
b) I don't like a person who is . . .
c) I like people who . . .
d) I can't stand it when . . .
e) It bothers me when someone . . .
f) My best friend is someone who . . .

4 PRONUNCIATION: Emphatic stress

1 We give words extra stress to show we feel strongly about something. Listen and practice these sentences.

> I **can't stand** it when people chew gum while they're talking!
> I think people who blow smoke in your face are **disgusting!**
> I **love** it when my mother bakes me a cherry pie!
> I **hate** people who are always late!

2 *Group work*   Now take turns reading the sentences you wrote in Exercise 3. Give extra stress to one word or phrase in each sentence.

5 IT TAKES ALL KINDS

1 Think of three qualities you like or dislike most in these people.

a) a roommate   *I can't stand a roommate who...*
b) a friend   *I think a friend should be ...*
c) a boss   *I like a boss who is ...*

2 *Group work*   Compare your opinions.

6 DO YOU HAVE A "TYPE A" OR "TYPE B" PERSONALITY?

Some doctors believe there are two main types of personalities: "Type A" and "Type B." Type A people are ambitious, aggressive, hardworking, and competitive; they are sometimes impatient and are often in a hurry.

Type B people are more relaxed and don't get bothered easily. Doctors say that because they are so hard driving, Type A personalities often suffer from stress and high blood pressure.

Pair work Take turns asking your partner these questions and check (✓) Yes or No. Is your partner a Type A or Type B personality? How about you?

		Yes	No			Yes	No
a)	Are you always in a hurry to finish things?	.....	.....	g)	Do you sometimes stop listening when people are talking to you?	.....	.....
b)	Are you ambitious and always looking for new challenges?	.....	.....	h)	Do you expect to be the best at everything you do?	.....	.....
c)	Are you often impatient with other people?	.....	.....	i)	Do you often interrupt people while they are speaking?	.....	.....
d)	Do you get upset when people are late for appointments?	.....	.....	j)	Do you think the best way to get a job done is to do it yourself?	.....	.....
e)	Do you often do two things at once, such as watching TV while eating?	.....	.....				
f)	Do you get upset easily when things go wrong?	.....	.....		**To score:** Six or more Yes answers = Type A; six or more No answers = Type B.		

7 LISTENING 🔊

Listen to three people talking. Do you think they have Type A or Type B personalities? Check (✓) the chart below and answer why.

	Type A	Type B	Why?
1) Judy			
2) Kenji			
3) George			

▶ **Interchange 1: Hidden truths**

Find out about some of your classmates' secrets. Turn to page 102.

8 SNAPSHOT

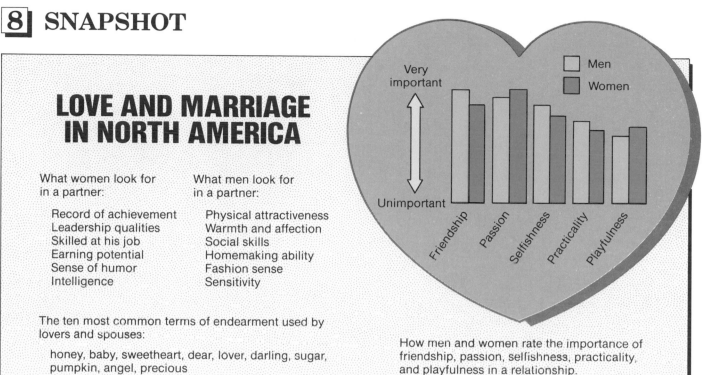

LOVE AND MARRIAGE IN NORTH AMERICA

What women look for in a partner:

Record of achievement
Leadership qualities
Skilled at his job
Earning potential
Sense of humor
Intelligence

What men look for in a partner:

Physical attractiveness
Warmth and affection
Social skills
Homemaking ability
Fashion sense
Sensitivity

The ten most common terms of endearment used by lovers and spouses:

honey, baby, sweetheart, dear, lover, darling, sugar, pumpkin, angel, precious

How men and women rate the importance of friendship, passion, selfishness, practicality, and playfulness in a relationship.

Discussion

What are the five things you look for the most in a partner?

Of the five things that are important in a relationship, which three are the most important to you?

Do you use similar terms of endearment in your language? What other terms are used?

9 CONVERSATION 📼

1 Listen.

Sue: Oh! Don't they make a perfect couple!
Tom: Yes, they really do. They're both so easygoing and sociable.
Sue: Where did they meet?
Tom: In Florida. Linda was teaching a computer course, and Bob was one of her students. But guess what! He failed the course!

2 Now listen to Sue and Tom describing how they met their best friends. Take notes.

Who are their best friends?
How did they meet?
What are their friends like?

3 *Role play*   Use your notes and role-play the conversation between Sue and Tom.

10 GRAMMAR FOCUS: Adverbial clauses of time 🔊

When you were in primary school, who was your favorite teacher?	**When I went to primary school,** my favorite teacher was Mrs. Sanchez.
Who was your best friend **when you were in junior high school?**	**When I was in junior high school,** my best friend was Tommy Wong.
How did you meet your best friend?	We met **while we were working at a fast food restaurant.**
Did you study English **when you were in college?**	Yes, I studied English **when I was in college.**

Pair work Take turns asking some of these questions. Then ask four more questions of your own.

When you were a child, . . .
While you were in primary school, . . .
When you were in high school, . . .
While you were in college, . . .

who was your best friend?	did you study English?
what was your favorite sport?	did you use to cut classes?
who was your favorite teacher?	did you have a girlfriend or boyfriend?
what was your best subject?	did you have a part-time job?

11 BEST FRIENDS

Pair work Take turns talking about your best friends. Ask questions like these.

Who is your best friend?
Where did you meet? How did you meet?
What is your friend like?
How is your friend similar to or different from you?
What do you like most about your friend?

12 WRITING

1 Write a composition about your best friend.

My best friend is Maria. She lives in my apartment building. We met one day while I was...

I really like Maria because she is very generous. She's a person who...

2 *Pair work* Exchange compositions. Read your partner's composition and then cover it. How much can you remember? Tell your partner.

13 READING: In good faith

1 Have you ever made friends while you were traveling? Have you ever lost anything or had anything stolen while you were traveling? What was it? Did you get it back?

2 Now read this story and then answer the questions below.

Tadatoyo Yamamoto, 44, is a Japanese businessman who visits the United States from time to time. While he was checking into a hotel on a recent visit to Chicago, he put his briefcase on the floor. A few minutes later, Mr. Yamamoto reached down for it, but someone had stolen it. Inside the briefcase were about $900 in Japanese currency, his passport, his credit cards, photos of his family, and his return ticket to Japan.

A few days later, Mr. Yamamoto returned to Tokyo, disappointed and disillusioned about the United States. But three weeks later, he received an envelope. There was no letter, but it contained his credit cards, his airline tickets, and other personal items. The return address gave the name of Mr. Joseph Loveras in Chicago. Not long after that, Mr. Yamamoto received another envelope sent by express delivery. Inside were money orders for more than $900. It also contained a letter from Mr. Loveras that said, "I hope this money order and the items . . . will restore your faith in the people of Chicago." Mr. Yamamoto was puzzled.

The next time he traveled to the United States, Mr. Yamamoto called on Mr. Loveras. Mr. Loveras was a 67-year-old disabled veteran with a total income of $493 a month.

He explained that he found the briefcase in a trash can while he was walking through a parking lot. For some reason, the thief had not discovered the money or the airline tickets in the top part of the briefcase and had just thrown the bag away. Mr. Loveras went to a bank and changed the money into money orders, and he spent his own money to send it to Japan. Mr. Yamamoto was very moved by Mr. Loveras's honesty. "I asked him why he would go to all the trouble to return everything to me. He told me that if he had not done it, it would have made him feel bad for the rest of his life." Now they have become friends, and Mr. Yamamoto visits Mr. Loveras every time he is in the United States.

a) How did Mr. Yamamoto lose his briefcase?
b) How did he get the contents back?
c) What kind of person is Mr. Loveras?
d) What would you have done if you had found the briefcase?

2 On the job

1 SNAPSHOT

People who quit their jobs each day in the U.S.: 60,000
People who are fired each day: 12,000
People who would like their boss's job: 29%
Teachers who wish they had chosen another career: 24%
People who have invented a job or degree for their
    résumés: 10%
Owners of small businesses who do not have a college
    degree: 76%

Discussion
Have you or has a family member ever quit a job? Why?
Would you like to exchange jobs with your boss? Why or why not?
What are five well-paid jobs in your country?

2 CONVERSATION

1 Listen.

A: So you're a journalist. That must be an exciting job.
B: It is, at times. It's certainly better than being a teacher!
A: Oh, really?
B: Yeah. I used to be a teacher, but I hated it! The worst thing about teaching is correcting homework. That's why I quit.
A: I guess you travel a lot now and meet lots of interesting people.
B: Yes, that's one of the best things about my job.
A: Sounds great. I wish I had a job like that.
B: Where do you work?
A: In an office. It's kind of boring. I'm stuck inside all day, and I have to work long hours.
B: Oh? What do you do?
A: I'm a vice president.

2 Which do you think is more interesting, being a teacher or being a journalist? Why?

3 *Role play* Now close your books and role-play the conversation using your own words.

8

3 GRAMMAR FOCUS: Comparisons 🔲

A lawyer is **better paid than** a teacher.

A lawyer earns **more than** a clerk.

Teaching is **more challenging than** office work.

Being an accountant is **as challenging as** being a teacher.

A teacher has **better benefits than** a journalist.

The best thing about being a teacher is the vacations.

A teacher is **not as well paid as** a lawyer.

A clerk **doesn't** earn **as much as** a lawyer.

Office work is **less challenging than** teaching.

Being a clerk is **not as challenging as** being a teacher.

A journalist has **worse benefits than** a teacher.

The worst thing about being a teacher is correcting homework.

A lawyer

1 Match the information to make sentences.

A

a) A high school teacher doesn't earn

b) Working on a construction site is more dangerous

c) The worst things about being a doctor

d) One of the best things about being a flight attendant

e) A taxi driver is not as well paid

B

.... is getting free air travel for yourself and your family.

.... as much as a doctor.

.... as an airline pilot.

.... are the long hours and having to work weekends and evenings.

.... than working in an office.

2 Now complete the phrases in column A with your own information. Then compare with a partner.

3 *Pair work* Compare these jobs. Use your own information.

a nurse and a doctor
a teacher and a student
a mechanic and an engineer
a pilot and a flight attendant

A teacher

4 PRONUNCIATION: Sentence stress 🔲

1 Listen to the stress in these sentences from the grammar box in Exercise 3.

A **lawyer** is **better paid** than a **teacher**.
A **teacher** is **not** as **well paid** as a **lawyer**.
A **lawyer** earns **more** than a **clerk**.
A **clerk doesn't** earn as **much** as a **lawyer**.

2 Now listen to the rest of the sentences. Mark the stressed words and then practice the sentences.

5 LISTENING 📼

1 Listen to Julia and Carlos talking about their new jobs and take notes. What do they like or dislike about them?

2 Listen again. How does Carlos's new job compare with his old one?

6 WORD POWER: Making a living

1 Put these words in the categories below. Then compare with a partner.

bonus   health insurance   pension plan
challenge   overtime pay   responsibility
commission   paid vacations   variety

Job satisfaction	Salary and earnings	Benefits

2 *Pair work*   Can you add five more words to the chart?

3 *Group work*   Can you think of (a) three jobs where you can get commissions, (b) three jobs that are challenging, and (c) three jobs that have a lot of responsibility?

7 THE RAT RACE

1 *Group work*   Choose three of these jobs and list three advantages and three disadvantages for each.

homemaker   teacher   taxi driver
traveling salesperson   construction worker   police officer

2 How interesting are the jobs above? Rank them from 1 to 6 (1 = most interesting). Then compare answers around the class.

8 CONVERSATION 🔊

1 Listen to Celia's interview at an employment agency.

A: When did you graduate, Celia?
B: I graduated last year.
A: I see. And what have you been doing since then?
B: Traveling mostly. I love to travel, but now I think it's time for me to get a job.
A: Uh-huh. Are you good at foreign languages?
B: Yes, I think so. I speak French and German, and I can speak a little Russian.
A: Mmm. What kind of job are you looking for?
B: Well, I'd like to have a job where I can use my writing skills. I love working with computers and organizing information. Also, I'd like to work in a large office, so that I'm around other people.
A: OK . . . Well, I think I have the perfect job for you!

2 *Pair work* Can you think of a good job for Celia?

3 *Role play* Close your books and have a conversation like the one above. Student A asks the questions, and Student B answers with real information.

9 LISTENING 🔊

1 Listen to two people being interviewed for jobs. Which job is each person applying for?

Looking for private detective. Agency needs sharp, young trainee for full-time position.	Spanish teacher needed for private language school. Native speaker with 2 years' experience preferred.	Vacancy in law office. Lawyer needed to work for an export company. Must know international law.	International tour guide. Immediate opening with large tour agency. Good salary/benefits.

2 Listen again and take notes. What does each job require?

10 GRAMMAR FOCUS: Adverbs of degree and adjectives 🔊

I can type **(very) well.**	I'm **very good** at typing.
I speak Spanish **pretty well.**	**good** at Spanish.
fairly well.	**fairly good** at languages.
I can type **a little.**	**pretty good** at speaking it.
I can't type **(very) well.**	**OK** at it.
I don't speak it **at all.**	I'm **not very good** at typing.
	terrible at it.

1 Put the words in B's answers in the correct order.
Then compare with a partner and practice the conversation.

a) A: How well can you write English?
   B: think write pretty I well English can I
b) A: Are you very good at math?
   B: math no terrible actually at I'm
c) A: Do you know how to use an adding machine?
   B: using good adding machine I'm yes an at
d) A: Are you good at keeping deadlines?
   B: at yeah deadlines good keeping I'm pretty
e) A: Do you get along well with people?
   B: very with usually yes get well along I people
f) A: Are you good at public speaking?
   B: at very I'm no it good not

2 *Pair work* Take turns asking the questions and giving your own
answers. Then ask four more questions.

11 PERSONNEL FILE

1 *Pair work* Take turns asking these questions and others of your own.

How many languages do you know?
How well do you (speak/write) . . .?
Are you good at sports?
How well can you swim?
What computer skills do you have?
Can you type?
Do you like working on a team?
Are you good at managing people?
How well can you work under pressure?
Are you punctual?

2 *Group work* Tell the group two
interesting things you learned about your partner.

12 WRITING

1 Prepare a self-profile. First, make notes about your educational
background, work experience, language skills, other skills,
and personal qualities. Then write a composition.

> I am a high school graduate. I graduated from
> Allen High School in 1991. Since then, I have
> worked at First Valley Bank. In my job, I am
> responsible for filing and general office work.
> I speak two languages. I am good at ...

2 *Pair work* Exchange your profiles and answer any
questions your partner may have.

▶ **Interchange 2:
I'd like that job!**

How well do you do at job
interviews? Turn to page
103 to find out.

13 READING: Stressed out

Does work or study sometimes cause you stress?
How does this stress affect you?
What do you do to help yourself relax?

Now read this article about job stress
and answer the questions below.

Stress on the job costs American companies as much as $150 billion a year in
lower productivity, unnecessary employee
sick leave, and higher medical costs.
Three-quarters of the office workers today
say they suffer from stress at work.
Recently, psychologists and doctors have
begun to study the problem more closely.
They have discovered that the most stress-
ful professions are those that involve dan-
ger and extreme pressure and those that
carry a lot of responsibility without much
control.

The signs of stress range from nervousness,
anger, and frequent illness to forgetfulness
and even mental problems. The best way
to deal with stress is through relaxation,
but sometimes the only answer is to fight
back or walk away.

Ten jobs with high stress	Some warning signs of stress	Some ways to cope with stress
inner-city high school teacher	intestinal distress	maintain a sense of humor
police officer	rapid pulse	meditate
miner	frequent illness	get a massage
air-traffic controller	persistent fatigue	exercise regularly
medical intern	irritability	eat more sensibly
stockbroker	nail biting	limit intake of alcohol and caffeine
journalist	lack of concentration	spend more time with family and friends
clerk in complaint department	increased use of alcohol and drugs	say no to the boss
waitress/waiter	hunger for sweets	quit your job
secretary		

a) Why do you think the jobs above often produce stress?
b) Do you show any of the warning signs when you are stressed?
c) How else do people sometimes react when they are under stress?
d) Which of the ways to cope listed above are most effective?
e) What are some other ways of coping with stress?

3 Destinations

1 SNAPSHOT

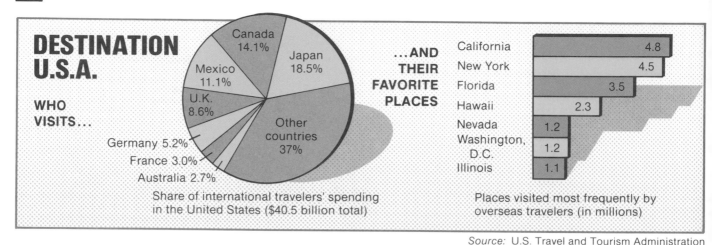

DESTINATION U.S.A.

WHO VISITS...

- Canada 14.1%
- Japan 18.5%
- Mexico 11.1%
- U.K. 8.6%
- Germany 5.2%
- France 3.0%
- Australia 2.7%
- Other countries 37%

Share of international travelers' spending in the United States ($40.5 billion total)

...AND THEIR FAVORITE PLACES

- California 4.8
- New York 4.5
- Florida 3.5
- Hawaii 2.3
- Nevada 1.2
- Washington, D.C. 1.2
- Illinois 1.1

Places visited most frequently by overseas travelers (in millions)

Source: U.S. Travel and Tourism Administration 1990 estimates

Discussion

Do many tourists visit your country every year? Where do they come from?

Which places do they like to visit?

What is the most interesting city in your country? Why?

Which places in the U.S. and Canada would you most like to visit? Why?

2 CONVERSATION 📼

1 Listen.

Andy: Whereabouts are you from, Carla?

Carla: I'm from Santa Fe, New Mexico.

Andy: Oh? What's it like there?

Carla: Well, it's a beautiful little tourist town, and the climate's great. Actually, it's a center for American Indian culture, and there are also lots of artists there. Georgia O'Keeffe, the famous painter, used to live there.

Andy: Really? It sounds like an interesting place! I'd love to go there sometime.

Carla: Yeah, you'd enjoy it, Andy.

2 Now listen to the rest of the conversation. Where is Andy from? What's it like there?

3 *Pair work* Now have a conversation like this about your hometown.

14

3 GRAMMAR FOCUS: Order of adjectives 📼

	Quality	Size	Age	Origin	Type	Noun
Santa Fe is a	beautiful	little			tourist	town.
Bruges is a	lovely		old		medieval	city.
Carmel is a	delightful			American	seaside	resort.

1 Put these adjectives in the correct order.

a) Kensington is a .... (London, old, fashionable) suburb.
b) Detroit is an .... (industrial, American, old) city.
c) Sorrento is a .... (charming, summer, Italian) resort about seventeen
   miles south of Naples.
d) Kingston is a .... (Canadian, university, medium-sized) town in Ontario.
e) Bali is a .... (tropical, little, fascinating) island in Indonesia.
f) Quebec City is a .... (charming, French-speaking, old) city in Canada.
g) My hometown is a .... (pleasant, farming, little) town about two hundred
   miles from here.

2 Now listen and check your answers.

3 *Pair work* Make sentences to describe four cities or places you
know. Then compare your sentences around the class.

4 LISTENING 📼

1 Listen to this talk on Madrid. Write
down one thing the speaker says on each of
these topics:

population   weather
industry   entertainment
life-style

2 *Pair work* Compare notes. How
much can you remember about Madrid?

5 A GREAT PLACE

1 *Pair work* Choose an interesting city or place to give a talk on.
Make notes about these or other topics.

cost of living   housing   location   size
employment   industry   population   weather

2 *Group work* Now give your talks and answer any questions.

6 WORD POWER: The weather

1 *Pair work* Look at these words that describe the weather. Can you add six more words to the list? Then compare with a partner.

| drought | hail | lightning | snow | summer | thunder | typhoon |
| flood | humidity | shower | storm | sun | tornado | wind |

2 *Pair work* Now make five sentences. Use two words from the list in each sentence.

There was a tornado in my hometown last summer.
When there is thunder, there is usually lightning.

7 CONVERSATION 📼

1 Listen.

A: I'm thinking about spending my vacation in southeast Asia, but I haven't decided where.
B: Oh? What kind of place are you looking for?
A: Somewhere with good weather, that's quiet and far away from the crowds.
B: Hmm, Phuket might be the place.
A: Phuket? Where's that?
B: In Thailand. It's a beautiful island with excellent beaches. I was there last summer. It's fantastic!
A: Sounds good. But what about the weather?
B: The weather is great. And there are plenty of cheap hotels along the beach.
A: It sounds just like the kind of place I'm looking for.

2 *Role play* Have a conversation like the one above. Use your own information.

16

8 PRONUNCIATION: Reduced forms of *there are / there is* 📼

1 Listen to how **there are** is usually pronounced.

There are excellent beaches.   **There are** lots of cheap flights.
There are hardly any tourists.

Now listen to how **there is** is usually pronounced.

There's great food in the local restaurants.   **There's** not much crime.
There's good weather at this time of the year.

2 Listen again and practice the sentences above.

---

9 GRAMMAR FOCUS: Quantifiers with countable and uncountable nouns 📼

With countable nouns	With uncountable nouns
There are **too many** tourists.	There is **too much** rain.
a few hostels.	**a little** pollution.
(very) few restaurants.	**(very) little** poverty.
not many beaches.	**not much** traffic.
plenty of parks.	**plenty of** sightseeing.
a lot of/lots of shops.	**a lot of/lots of** crime.
(not) enough hotels.	**(not) enough** industry.
hardly any thunderstorms.	**hardly any** humidity.
no typhoons.	**no** public housing.

Plenty of snow

1 Complete these sentences with phrases from the grammar box. Then compare with a partner. More than one answer is possible.

a) There .... snow in the winter, but there .... rain in the summer.
b) Unemployment is high in the north of the country because there .... industry there.
c) It's best to visit in April or May. There .... tourists then, and it's easy to get a hotel room.
d) Unfortunately, there .... pollution because there .... factories in the city.
e) If there .... rain in the spring, then we often have a drought in July.
f) It's a safe city because there .... crime.

2 *Pair work* Use phrases from the grammar box to describe the city or town you are in. Write six sentences about these or other topics: **tourist attractions, hotels, transportation, industries, shopping, weather.**

3 *Class activity* Take turns reading some of your sentences to the class. Do your classmates agree?

A lot of pollution

10 LISTENING 🔲

1 Listen to people talking about five different places and circle **T** (true) or **F** (false).

a) T F There are very few tourist attractions.
b) T F There is a lot of poverty there.
c) T F There is plenty of good public transportation.
d) T F There are a lot of tourists in the city.
e) T F There is too much rain in the winter.

2 Listen again. For the sentences you marked false, give the correct information.

---

11 WRITING

1 Think of a city you would like to write about (but not the city you are in). Then make notes on topics like these:

cost of living   housing   location   size
employment   industry   population   weather

2 Now use your notes to write a composition of at least three paragraphs.

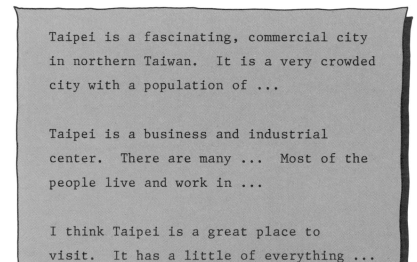

```
Taipei is a fascinating, commercial city
in northern Taiwan.  It is a very crowded
city with a population of ...

Taipei is a business and industrial
center.  There are many ...  Most of the
people live and work in ...

I think Taipei is a great place to
visit.  It has a little of everything ...
```

3 *Pair work* Exchange compositions. Does your partner have any questions or comments?

▶ **Interchange 3: The best and the worst**

Be a city critic. Turn to page 104.

12 READING: Discovering Australia

Read these two passages and then answer the questions below.

Is Australia the world's largest island or its smallest continent? Actually, it's both. In fact, Australia is the only country that is also a continent. Although roughly the size of the United States mainland, Australia has a population of about 16.5 million people. That makes this island nation one of the least densely populated countries.

What ethnic groups make up the Australian population? The majority of Australians are of English, Irish, Italian, Greek, Dutch, and Polish descent. However, over the past 50 years, some 4 million people from more than 120 countries have made Australia their home. This includes a large number of Asian and African immigrants. About one percent of the population is Aborigine. The Aboriginal people were the first settlers in Australia. They came from Asia about 40,000 years ago.

In addition to being the smallest continent, Australia is also the driest inhabited continent. Lush green pastures may be typical in sheep farming areas (there are, by the way, more sheep than people in Australia). However, much of the land, particularly in the Outback, is so arid that people are unable to live on it in its undeveloped state. That explains why most Australians live in metropolitan areas, many of which line the coast, and why Australia is considered one of the world's more urbanized countries.

Make friends with a koala at one of our wildlife parks. Explore the lush, green bushland areas of the Blue Mountains. Marvel at the coral of our magnificent Great Barrier Reef. Or be awed by our ancient landscapes and strange land formations. Whatever your interests, Australia has what you're looking for.

Lining our coast are some of the world's most sophisticated cities – like Melbourne, Brisbane, and Sydney. There you can enjoy all the best in food, fashion, the arts, theater, and sports. But you won't want to miss the wonders of the vast and amazing Outback or the peaceful beauty of the Bush. Australia has a variety of unique trees, plants, and wildlife. Discover them at any of our magnificent wildlife preserves and parks.

No matter where you go in Australia, you'll find something to delight you. So surf or ski, relax on our beautiful beaches, see Aboriginal rock art painted thousands of years ago, and meet interesting people. Don't wait. It's always a good time to visit Australia.

a) Which passage would you expect to find in a travel brochure? Why?
b) Which passage states only facts about Australia?
c) What are four facts about Australia?
d) What are four opinions?
e) Why would someone want to vacation in Australia?
f) Why do most Australians live in cities or towns?

Review of Units 1-3

1 What does it take?

1 *Group work* What are the four most important skills you need for these jobs?

a director of a company   a secretary
a doctor   a waiter/waitress

Talk about them like this:

A: To be a doctor, you need to be good at caring for people.
B: Yes, and you should . . .
C: You must . . .
D: And you have to . . .

2 *Class activity* Compare your suggestions.

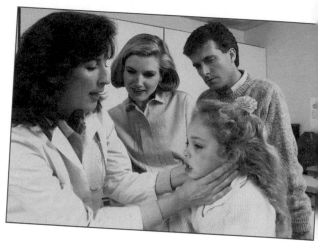

2 Career counseling

1 *Role play* Student A is a career counselor; Student B is a college senior who has not decided on a career yet. Cover each other's information and use the cues below.

Student A: Career counselor
Greet the student.
Ask about these things:
– educational background
– personal qualities
– the kinds of work he or she would be interested in (for example, office work, sales work, business, industry)
Suggest one or two careers he or she might like to think about.

Student B: College senior
Introduce yourself.
Talk about these things:
– your major and educational background
– your language skills and other skills
– your personal qualities
– the kinds of work you are interested in
Ask for suggestions about different kinds of careers or jobs.
Talk about a job that interests you.

2 Now change roles and partners and try the role play again.

3 Listening 🎦

Listen to three conversations. Check (✓) the two adjectives that best describe George, Karen, and Pam.

	Ambitious	Helpful	Honest	Proud	Selfish	Unreliable
#1 George						
#2 Karen						
#3 Pam						

4 Haiku

Golden Gate Bridge, San Francisco

A haiku is a Japanese poem of three lines that has:

5 syllables in the first line   *Beautiful city*

7 syllables in the second   *Lovely bridge over the bay*

5 syllables in the third   *I left my heart there.*

Write a haiku about someone you know or a place you like. Then read your poem to the class.

5 Going places

Pair work   Take turns asking each other about an interesting city or place you have visited. Use these questions or other questions of your own.

What's an interesting city or place you have visited?
How big is it?
What's the weather like there?
Is there much unemployment?
And what about industry?
What's the transportation like?
Is there any pollution there?

What's the cost of living like?
What kind of housing do people have?
Are rents expensive?
What can you do there?
Are there many tourist attractions?
What's good to buy there?
What's the nightlife like?
What else do you like about it?

4 What a story!

1 SNAPSHOT

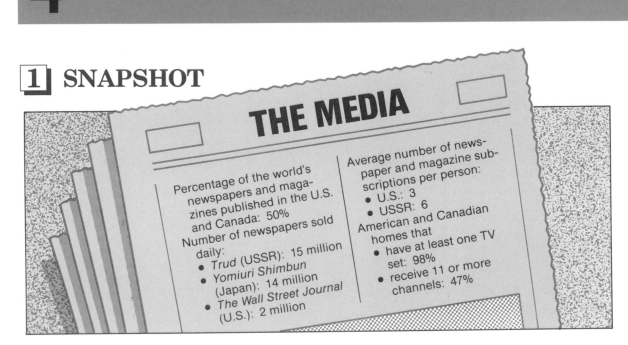

THE MEDIA

Percentage of the world's newspapers and magazines published in the U.S. and Canada: 50%

Number of newspapers sold daily:
- Trud (USSR): 15 million
- Yomiuri Shimbun (Japan): 14 million
- The Wall Street Journal (U.S.): 2 million

Average number of newspaper and magazine subscriptions per person:
- U.S.: 3
- USSR: 6

American and Canadian homes that
- have at least one TV set: 98%
- receive 11 or more channels: 47%

Discussion

Do you get your daily news from TV, radio, or newspapers?

How many hours do you watch television every week?

How many newspapers and magazines do you subscribe to or read regularly? What are they?

2 LISTENING

1 Match each headline with the beginning of a news story below.

Emergency on Flight 85

Stockbroker's Phone Never Stops Ringing

Clerk pays high price to get to work on time

a) A Miami man was fined $4,000 yesterday for stealing an ambulance.

b) A woman who lost $50,000 on the stock market was arrested in a public phone booth today.

c) A 727 airplane made an unexpected landing yesterday.

d) A man who tried to break into a house on Friday got stuck in a chimney for fifty hours.

2 Now listen to a news broadcast about each headline and take notes. Then discuss these questions with a partner.

a) Why did the plane make an emergency landing? Was anyone injured?

b) Why was the woman arrested? Why was she angry?

c) Why did the Miami man steal the ambulance? Who stopped him?

22

3 DID YOU HEAR ABOUT . . .?

1 *Group work* What are three news events that have occurred recently? Talk about them like this:

A: I heard on the news that there was a bank robbery downtown yesterday.
B: Did you hear about the big earthquake yesterday? Luckily, no one was killed.
C: I read in the paper that . . .

2 *Class activity* Now groups describe their news events to the class and answer any questions.

4 GRAMMAR FOCUS: Questions with past tense

Yes/No questions	Wh-questions
Did the police catch the robber?	Who did the police arrest?
Was the man a thief?	Who robbed the store?
Was anyone hurt?	Where was the money hidden?
Were the passengers injured?	What happened to the car?

Read this story and write six past tense questions about it.

A man who tried to break into a house on Friday got stuck in a chimney for fifty hours. The owner of the house returned after a weekend vacation and heard a strange noise in her chimney. She called the police, who found a neighbor stuck upside-down in the chimney. He had climbed onto the roof and was trying to enter the house through the chimney when he got stuck. The man claimed he had returned home drunk, lost his key, and thought this was his house. After the police got him out of the chimney, they arrested him.

5 PRONUNCIATION: Reduced and blended forms in Wh-questions ▭

1 Listen to the reduced and blended words in these questions.

Where was the woman arrested?   **Why did the** plane land?
Why was she angry?   **How did they** find him?
Where were the police?   **Where did they** find the woman?

2 *Pair work* Now cover the story in Exercise 4 and take turns asking the questions you wrote. Use reduced forms.

6 WORD POWER: Verbs

1 Find six pairs of opposites in the list below. Then write down the past tense form of each verb and compare with a partner.

admit	deny	leave	release
arrest	enter	lend	send
borrow	fail	receive	succeed

2 *Pair work* Make four more pairs of opposites using other verbs.
Then compare your list in a group.
What are the past tense forms of these verbs?

3 Write six sentences in the past tense using any of the verbs from part 1 or 2.

7 THAT'S INCREDIBLE!

1 *Group work* Choose one of these headlines and make up an interesting story about it. One student starts the story. Then another student tells what happened next and so on.

THIS WEEK'S SIGHTING

MRS. ELLEN TRASKIN OF NEW HOPE, PA., POINTS TO SPOT WHERE SHE SAW ELVIS PRESLEY EMERGE FROM A FLYING SAUCER. (NOTE MYSTERIOUS GUITAR-SHAPED CLOUD ABOVE SITE.)

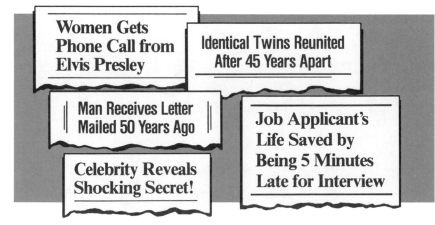

Women Gets Phone Call from Elvis Presley

Identical Twins Reunited After 45 Years Apart

Man Receives Letter Mailed 50 Years Ago

Job Applicant's Life Saved by Being 5 Minutes Late for Interview

Celebrity Reveals Shocking Secret!

2 *Class activity* Groups take turns telling their stories.
Other students ask questions. Which group has the best story?

8 CONVERSATION 🔊

1 Listen.

A: You know, I had a really strange dream last night.
B: Oh, yeah? What was it about?
A: Well, I dreamed that I was driving in the country late at night when I saw a UFO land on the road in front of me.
B: And then what happened?
A: Well, first, I got out of my car. While I was standing there, this strange green creature came out of the UFO. I tried to run away, but I couldn't move. Then, as it was coming nearer, it put out its hand and touched my face. It felt wet and horrible!
B: Ugh! And . . .?
A: And then I woke up and found my cat on my pillow. It was licking my face!

2 *Pair work* Now close the book. How much of the dream can you remember?

3 *Group work* Take turns talking about a dream you once had.

9 GRAMMAR FOCUS: Past tense and past continuous 🔊

Past tense	Past continuous
I **drove** in the country.	I **was driving** in the country when I saw a UFO.
I **stood** there.	While I **was standing** there, this strange creature came out.
It **came** nearer.	As it **was coming** nearer, it put out its hand.

1 Put one verb in the past tense and one verb in the past continuous. Then practice the sentences.

a) I .... (have) dinner at a restaurant downtown last night when the actor Eddie Murphy .... (come) in and sat at the next table.
b) I .... (find) this ring as I .... (walk) through the park today.
c) While I .... (get) my hair cut, I .... (fall) asleep.
d) The workers .... (uncover) some old coins while they .... (work) on the building site.
e) We .... (see) the Prime Minister drive by while we .... (wait) for the bus this morning.

2 Complete these sentences with information of your own. Then compare with a partner.

a) One time, when I was driving on the freeway, . . .
b) I was visiting a friend a few years ago when . . .
c) While I was having a meal in a restaurant last week, . . .
d) Once, as I was riding in an elevator, . . .
e) I was walking downtown recently when . . .

10 LISTENING 📼

Listen to three people describing dreams they had and take notes.

Where were they?
What were they doing?
What happened?

11 A HAPPY ENDING

1 *Pair work* Choose one of the dreams in Exercise 10. How do you think it ended? Make up an interesting ending for it.

2 *Group work* Take turns telling how the dreams ended.

12 WRITING

1 Make up an interesting dream like the ones in Exercise 10 or write about a dream you really had.

| Where were you? | Who else was in the dream? |
| What happened? | How did the dream end? |

2 *Pair work* Now read about each other's dream.

▶ **Interchange 4: A double ending**

Solve a mystery! Students A and B look at page 105, and Students C and D at page 106.

13 READING: In the news

1 Read this story from the *National Examiner* newspaper and then answer these questions.

Why did aliens bring Bigfoot to Earth?
Where have many Bigfoot sightings taken place?
What does Bigfoot look like?
What were Mr. Sherry and Mr. Bosak doing when they saw Bigfoot?

Aliens Brought Bigfoot to Earth Claim UFO Experts

By EDWARD REYNOLDS

BIGFOOT creatures could be experimental animals that UFO aliens brought to Earth in order to test the environment before colonizing.

That's the incredible explanation given by Walt H. Andrus Jr., international director of the Mutual UFO Network based in Seguin, Texas.

And it is one shared by top UFOlogist Timothy Green Beckley, editor of the New York–based magazine *UFO Universe*. He says that there is a definite link between Bigfoot and UFO sightings, especially through Ohio, Pennsylvania, and New Jersey.

More than 600 people in Pennsylvania alone reported seeing UFOs or strange creatures like Big-

foot in 1988, according to a report published in *The Pittsburgh Press*.

A 67-year-old disabled army veteran from Wilpen, Pennsylvania, tells of a chilling encounter he had with a Bigfoot while on a fishing trip at Loyalhanna Creek, the site of numerous UFO sightings.

Sam Sherry says he stood within 20 feet of the beast, which he estimates weighed 700 pounds and stood six and a half feet tall with arms nearly down to its ankles.

Sherry claims the creature put one arm on his shoulder and another on his back as he turned to get in his car. Fortunately, he says, he was able to drive away.

Beckley says one of the most sensational Bigfoot sightings of recent times places the creature inside a UFO, and is verified by an

area investigator for the National Investigations Committee on Aerial Phenomena.

According to Beckley, University of Wisconsin professor J. M. Bostrack says that after a number of interviews with farmer Frederick Bosak he is convinced of the elderly man's sincerity.

Bosak claims he encountered a transparent UFO on the side of the road while driving toward his farm. He pulled alongside the craft and peered inside.

The Wisconsin farmer was quoted as saying: "All I know for sure is that he had thick reddish-brown hair covering his face and arms. This heavy layer of hair appeared to extend downward to the region of his chest . . ."

He added: "The eyes – I doubt frankly if I'll ever be able to erase them from my memory. They were big and round, really protruding."

Drawing reprinted courtesy Omni Magazine © 1990.

aliens: creatures from other planets
Bigfoot: a half-man, half-animal creature from
   prehistoric times that some people believe still
   lives in remote parts of North America
UFO: unidentified flying object
UFOlogist: someone who studies UFOs

2 Group work
Do you believe the stories told by Mr. Sherry and Mr. Bosak?
Can you think of any other explanations for what they say happened?
Have you heard of similar stories?

5 Could you do me a favor?

1 SNAPSHOT

JUST SAY NO

In some countries, people don't like to say no to a request. They avoid saying no by:

1 remaining silent
2 saying something vague or unclear
3 changing the topic
4 ending the conversation without answering the request
5 giving a false excuse
6 delaying a reply to the request
7 saying, "Yes, but..."

Discussion

Do people in your country use these ways of saying no? Which are the most common?

How would you decline these requests without saying no?

Could I borrow your car?
Can you lend me $100?
Could you please help me move to my new apartment on Sunday?
Do you want to see a movie tonight?

2 LISTENING 📼

1 Listen to three telephone conversations. Write down what each caller wants. Does the other person agree to the request? Check (✓) Yes or No.

	Request	*Yes*	*No*
a) Tina			
b) Mike			
c) Bill			

2 *Pair work*   Now role-play the telephone conversations.

3 PRONUNCIATION: Blended consonants 📼

When the sounds /t/, /d/, /k/, /g/, /p/, and /b/ come at the end of a word
and the next word begins with a consonant, the first consonant is
blended with the following consonant. Listen to the blended consonants
in these sentences. Then practice them.

Len**d m**e your bla**ck b**ag.   I don'**t l**ike **p**eople asking me for money.

Do you wan**t that m**agazine?   Do you nee**d that p**encil?

As**k B**ob **t**o si**t b**ehin**d m**e.   Would you min**d g**iving me tha**t** re**d b**ook?

---

4 GRAMMAR FOCUS: Requests with modals
and *if*-clauses 📼

Less formal	**Can** you please lend me $100?
↑	**Could** you let me use your car?
	Would you be able to mail this letter?
	Would you mind letting me use your Walkman?
	Would it be OK **if I borrowed your car?**
↓	Would you mind **if I used it?**
Most formal	I wonder **if you'd mind lending me your cassette player.**

1 *Pair work* Make requests with
modals or *if*-clauses using the cues below.
Then practice them.

a) You want to borrow someone's typewriter.
   A: *Would you mind . . .*
   B: Sorry. It's not working right.

b) You want someone to drive you to the
   airport.
   A: . . .
   B: OK. What time?

c) You want someone to help you move on
   Saturday.
   A: . . .
   B: Sure, that'll be fine, but I'm only free in the
      afternoon.

d) You want someone to lend you a camera.
   A: . . .
   B: Gee, I'm sorry. I'm going to use it later.

e) You want to use someone's telephone.
   A: . . .
   B: All right. Go ahead!

2 Write five requests like the ones above using modals and *if*-clauses.

3 *Group work* Now practice your requests. Others accept or decline.
Pay attention to blended consonants.

5 WRITING: Would you mind . . .?

1 Write a note to a friend or classmate asking for several favors and explain why you need help.

> Bob,
>
> I'm taking my boss and her husband out to dinner on Saturday, and I want to make a good impression. Would you mind if I borrowed your car? I promise to drive very carefully. And I wonder if you'd mind lending me that red bow tie of yours. Could you let me know as soon as possible? Thanks!
>
> Henry

2 *Pair work*   Exchange notes and write a reply accepting or declining the requests.

> Henry,
> Of course you can borrow my car on Saturday. You can pick it up at . . . About my red bow tie, I'd like to lend it to you but...
>
> Bob

6 WORD POWER: Adjectives and adverbs

1 Complete this chart.

Adjective	Adverb	Adjective	Adverb
angry	*angrily*		nervously
brave		quick	
	desperately		quietly
drunken		romantic	
	excitedly		slowly
loud		soft	

2 *Pair work*   Take turns reading this telephone conversation six different ways (for example, angrily, quietly, romantically).

A: What time shall we meet?
B: Let's meet at midnight.
A: Your place or mine?
B: Yours.

3 *Class activity*   Pairs read the conversation aloud. The class guesses how they are reading it (for example, angrily, drunkenly, loudly).

7 CONVERSATION 📼

1 Listen.

A: Hello?
B: Hello. Can I speak to Sophia, please?
A: I'm sorry, she's not in right now. Would you like to leave a message?
B: Yes, please. This is Harry. Would you tell her that Tony's having a party on Saturday?
A: Sure.
B: And please ask her if she'd like to go with me.
A: All right, Peter. I'll give her the message.
B: No, this is Harry, not Peter!
A: Oh, sorry.
B: By the way, who's Peter?

> Sophia,
> Harry called.
> Tony is having
> a party on Saturday.
> Would you like to
> go with him?
> — mom

2 *Pair work* Close your books and role-play the conversation. Make up your own messages.

8 GRAMMAR FOCUS: Indirect requests 📼

Statements & imperatives	Indirect requests
Tony is having a party.	Could you tell her that Tony's having a party?
Call me at five.	Would you ask Yoko to call me at five?
Don't be late.	Can you tell Harry not to be late?

Yes/No questions	Indirect requests
Is Ann free on Friday?	Can you ask Ann if she's free on Friday?
Does she have my number?	Could you ask her if she has my number?
Can she bring some tapes?	Would you ask her if she can bring some tapes?
Will he be there?	Please ask him if he'll be there.

Wh-questions	Indirect requests
When is Sophia going?	Can you ask Sophia when she's going?
When does the party start?	Could you ask him when the party starts?
What should we bring?	Would you ask her what we should bring?

1 Put the words in these requests in the correct order. Then compare with a partner.

a) you he class ask me can Don would after meet if ?
b) telephone you your could me number give ?
c) Susan ask Walkman would my return you to ?
d) noise tell so make Vera to you can much not ?
e) the ask class you starts teacher time what party could the ?

2 Now write five indirect requests you would like a classmate to ask other students.

3 *Class activity* Exchange requests. Go around the class and make the requests.

Amy's requests

Would you ask Antonio not to make so much noise?

> A: Antonio, Amy says please don't make so much noise.
> B: Oh, sorry.

Could you ask Julie to lend me $20?

> A: Julie, can you lend Amy $20?
> B: Tell her I'm broke this week.

4 *Pair work* Now tell your partner what each person said.

Antonio said he was sorry.
Julie said that she was broke this week.

---

9 LISTENING 🔊

Listen to three people leaving telephone messages. Write each message down.

---

10 WOULD YOU LIKE TO LEAVE A MESSAGE?

1 Make up a message for a classmate.

2 *Pair work* Take turns making phone calls and leaving messages.

A: Hello?
B: Hello. Can I speak to . . .?
A: I'm sorry, . . . not in. Would you like to leave a message?
B: Yes, please . . .

> ▶ **Interchange 5:**
> **You must be kidding!**
> How good are you at giving excuses? Turn to page 107 and find out.

11 READING: Strange messages

1 Read these true stories and make up a good title for each one.

1 One night in 1828, the captain of a ship crossing the Atlantic Ocean was in his cabin when suddenly a man stepped into the room. The captain had never seen the man before. The man said nothing, but he wrote a message on the wall of the cabin and then disappeared. The message said, "Turn the ship and sail to the northwest." The captain was surprised but decided to follow the stranger's instructions. A few hours later, he saw a small ship ahead that was sinking. The captain asked his crew to see what had happened. They only found one person on board the ship. It was the same man the captain had seen in his cabin. The man explained he had just awakened from a deep sleep. In his sleep, he dreamed that he was going to be rescued.

2 In 1956, a young Swedish sailor on a ship at sea became bored. He wrote a message and put it in a bottle. The message gave his name and address and asked any pretty girl who found it to write to him. Two years later, an Italian fisherman found the bottle and showed the message to his daughter. Just for a joke, she wrote to the sailor. He replied, and soon they started writing to each other regularly. Then they decided to meet. Shortly after their first meeting, the sailor and the fisherman's daughter got married.

3 Abraham Lincoln, the sixteenth president of the United States, may have received a message about his own death in a dream. One night in 1865, he had a strange dream. He dreamed he was inside the White House. A group of people were standing around a coffin in the East Room of the White House. Many of them were crying. "Who is dead?" he asked. "The president," someone answered. "He was killed by an assassin." A few days after this, on April 14th, Lincoln was shot and killed while he was watching a play at Ford's Theater in Washington, D.C.

2 *Pair work* Find the best place in each passage for these sentences.

Story #1: So he turned the ship to the northwest.
Story #2: So he decided to have some fun.
Story #3: Later, his body was taken to the East Room of the White House.

3 Have you (or has anyone you know) ever received a message in an unusual way? How? What was the message?

6 Comparatively speaking

1 SNAPSHOT

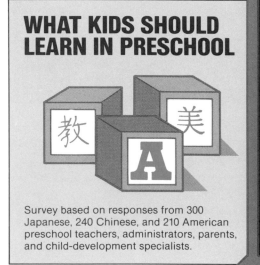

WHAT KIDS SHOULD LEARN IN PRESCHOOL

Survey based on responses from 300 Japanese, 240 Chinese, and 210 American preschool teachers, administrators, parents, and child-development specialists.

	JAPAN	CHINA	U.S.
Perseverance	2%	13%	3%
Cooperation	30%	37%	32%
Concern for others	31%	4%	5%
Creativity	9%	17%	6%
Reading and math skills	0%	6%	1%
Self-confidence	11%	6%	34%
Art, music, and dance	0.3%	1%	1%
Communication skills	1%	4%	8%
Physical skills	0.3%	1%	1%
Health and hygiene	14%	11%	1%
Gentleness	0%	0%	0%

Discussion
What do you think children should learn in preschool? Rank five things from the list above.

What else should kids learn in preschool?

2 CONVERSATION 📼

1 Listen.

Ann: Would you rather send your children to a public or a private school?

Tom: Mmm, I'd rather send them to a public school, I think.

Ann: Oh, why?

Tom: Well, it's cheaper for one thing . . .

Ann: Yes, but do you think the teachers are as good in the public schools?

Tom: Oh, yeah, I went to a public high school, and I had very good teachers there.

2 Now listen to the rest of the conversation. Does Ann prefer public or private schools? Why?

3 Which do you prefer, public or private schools? Have a conversation like the one above using your own information.

3 GRAMMAR FOCUS: *Would rather* and *prefer* 📼

Would you **rather send** your children to a public or a private school? **I'd rather send** them to a public school because it's cheaper.	Do you **prefer teaching** children or adults? **I prefer teaching** adults because they are easier to teach.

Complete these questions with the correct form: "Would you rather . . .?" *or* "Do you prefer . . .?"

a) . . . going to a daytime or an evening class?
b) . . . studying in a class or with a private tutor?
c) . . . study English in Australia or Canada?
d) . . . go to a community college or a university?
e) . . . major in the humanities or the sciences?

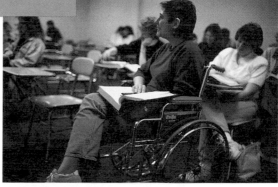

---

4 PRONUNCIATION: Intonation in questions of choice 📼

1 Listen to the intonation in questions where there is a choice.

Would you rather send your children to a public or a private school?

Do you prefer teaching children or adults?

Would you rather listen to classical music, pop, or jazz?

2 Now listen to the questions you completed in Exercise 3 and practice them. Then take turns asking and answering the questions.

---

5 PERSONAL PREFERENCES

1 *Pair work* Take turns asking these questions. Give reasons for your answers.

a) Would you rather live in the city or the suburbs?
b) Do you prefer traveling by air, train, or bus?
c) Would you rather work for someone else or be self-employed?
d) Do you prefer reading novels, newspapers, or magazines?

2 Now write questions about these topics. Then take turns asking your questions in groups.

games	marriage	music	travel
hobbies	movies	sports	work

Do you prefer playing video games or cards?

6 LISTENING 📼

1 Rita is talking to a friend.
What kind of work would she prefer?

a) .... work for the government
.... work for a company

b) .... work in an office
.... get a job that involves travel

c) .... earn a salary
.... work for a commission

2 Now listen again.
What reasons does Rita give for her choices?

▶ **Interchange 6:
Shopping survey**
Do you have spending preferences?
Find out by turning to page 108.

7 WORD POWER: Education

1 *Pair work* Write these words on the chart below.

botany   kindergarten   ceramics   physics
dressmaking   literature   philosophy   preschool

Schools	Arts and crafts	Humanities	Sciences

2 Now add three more words to each category.

8 CONVERSATION 🔲

1 Listen.

A: Is the education system in Britain the same as in the United States, Alex?
B: Well, it's fairly similar, but in most of the country we don't have separate junior and senior high schools. We just have secondary schools.
A: Oh? And how old are children when they enter secondary school?
B: Well, most kids enter when they're eleven. Then all students continue till they're sixteen, and many continue until they're eighteen.

2 Now listen to the rest of the conversation and take notes. What does Alex say about public schools in Britain?

3 *Pair work* How much can you remember about the education system in Britain (without using your book or notes)?

9 GRAMMAR FOCUS: Quantifiers 🔲

All students go to school till they are sixteen.	**Both** American **and** British students take national exams.
Most (students) study math.	**Neither** teachers **nor** students wear uniforms.
Many (students) take a foreign language in high school.	
A lot of colleges have dorms.	**Not all** primary schools teach foreign languages.
Some colleges are very expensive.	**Not many** children like homework.
Few schools have Saturday classes.	**No** colleges provide free lunches.
A few colleges teach German.	**None** of the private schools is cheap.

SNAP!
SNAP!

MICHIGAN

PSYCHOLOGY
Murray Levine

1 Complete these statements about your city (or town) or country and then compare with a partner.

a) In my country, most students . . .
b) Both public and private schools . . .
c) A lot of young people these days . . .
d) Not many stores . . .
e) Most banks . . .
f) Few factories . . .
g) All government employees . . .

2 *Pair work* Now make eight statements using phrases from the grammar box.

10 WHAT'S THE DIFFERENCE?

1 *Group work* Can you find three similarities and three differences between:

a) being a student and working full-time?
b) living in a large city and in a small town?
c) working for yourself and for someone else?

A: I think that being a student and working full-time have a lot in common. For one thing, most students . . .
B: Well, I agree. They are fairly similar. For example, both . . .
C: Actually, I don't think they have much in common because . . .

2 *Class activity* Groups compare their ideas.

11 LISTENING 🔊

1 *Pair work* What are some of the differences between being married and being single? Think of at least five differences.

2 Now listen to Sam and Charlie talking.

What does Sam like about being married?
What does Charlie like about being single?
Do they mention any of the things you talked about?

12 WRITING: Comparisons

1 Write about one of the things you discussed in Exercise 10. First make notes about these topics.

the differences   the similarities   your preference

2 Then use your notes to write a composition with three paragraphs. Start the first paragraph like this:

> There are several differences between being a student and working full-time. First, a lot of students . . .

3 *Pair work* Exchange compositions. Do you agree with your partner?

13 READING: A day at Dong-feng

Are there preschools or kindergartens in your country? What kinds of things do children do and learn there?

1 Now read about a preschool in China.

Dong-feng (East Wind) Kindergarten is a preschool run by a city in southwest China. It has 270 three-to six-year-old children and 60 staff members. Three-quarters of Dong-feng's children are day students who attend school from about 8 A.M. to 6 P.M., Monday through Saturday. The others are boarding students who go home only on Wednesday evenings and on weekends.

On a typical day, school starts at 7:30 A.M. with a breakfast of steamed buns. After breakfast, when the day students arrive, the teachers lead the children in morning exercises followed by a song. Then the children sit down and the teachers hand out wooden blocks.

Ms. Xiang says: "Just pay attention to the picture of the building and build it. We must use our minds, right? Build according to order." The children begin to work. Ms. Wang says: "Keep still! There is no need to talk while you are working."

At 10:00 it's time for the children to go to the bathroom. After that, they play a game of tag. At 10:45, it's bath time for the boarding students. Three or four at a time, the children bathe in large tubs. The children return to the classroom, and Ms. Wang drills them in addition and subtraction.

Later, lunch is delivered from the central kitchen. Ms. Xiang reminds the children to eat in

silence and not to waste any food. After lunch, it's time to go to the dormitory for a nap. Nap time lasts from noon to 2:30. While the children rest, the teachers catch up on paperwork, eat, and relax in the classroom next door.

After returning to their classroom, the children are taught to recite a story. Then they move outside for some relay races. At 5 P.M., the children have supper – a meal of meat, vegetables, and rice. At 6 P.M., the parents arrive to pick up their children. Inside, the boarders listen to music before getting ready for bed. By 7:45, the children are all in bed, and by 8:00 all are quiet and appear to be asleep.

2 *Group work* Which of these words do you think best describe a day at the preschool?

busy	challenging	fun	organized
carefree	disciplined	hectic	relaxing

What do you think the children learn at the school? How similar is this preschool to those in your country?

Review of Units 4-6

1 Headlines

Group work   What was the most interesting or unusual news story in your newspaper this week? Tell the group about it.

The most interesting story I read was about a woman who . . .   *(or)*
I read an unusual story about . . .

The rest of the group asks questions.

Where did . . . take place?	Why did . . .?
What happened?	Did they . . .?
How did . . .?	Who found . . .?

Woman with psychic powers helps police solve crime

Mrs. Sandy Starlight, who is well known for her powers of extra- "I've helped the police solve three crimes this year," said Mrs. Star-

2 The good and the bad

Group work   Read the questions below and then talk about them.

a) During the last four weeks, did anyone do something that made you feel good? What was it? What happened?
b) Has anything happened lately that made you feel bad? What was it? What happened?
c) Have you done anything in the last few weeks that made someone else feel good? What did you do?

Example:
It was my birthday last Tuesday. Some friends took me out to dinner after class. They took me to a very nice French restaurant. Afterwards, we went to a bar and sang a lot of old songs. We had a great time!

3 Listening ▭

Listen and choose the correct response.

a) .... Sure! I'd be glad to.
.... Yes, I'll tell her.
.... Sorry, I'm not free then.

b) .... Gee, I'm sorry.
.... OK, what time?
.... OK, I'll give him the message.

c) .... Well, actually, I'd like it back. Some friends are coming over tonight.
.... Sorry, it's in the repair shop.
.... Sure, I'll ask her.

d) .... Sorry, I'm still using it.
.... Yes, please.
.... Sure. Would a check be OK?

4 I wonder if you'd . . .

1 *Role play* Work in pairs and cover each other's information.

Student A

You are planning a class party at your house. Think of three things you need a classmate to help you with (for example, bring music/food/games; give someone a ride).

Now call a classmate and ask for help:
  Hi, Dave. I'm calling about the party. I wonder if you'd mind . . .

Finish the conversation like this:
  Well, thanks for your help. See you on Saturday!

Student B

A classmate is planning a party and calls you for help. Agree to help with some of the things, but not everything.

2 Now change partners and roles, and try the role play again.

5 What works for you?

1 What do you do to help you improve your English? Circle your preferences.

a) When you make a mistake in English, would you rather someone (1) corrected you immediately or (2) just ignored it?
b) When you hear a new word in English, do you prefer (1) writing it down or (2) trying to remember it?
c) If you don't understand what someone says, do you prefer (1) asking the person to repeat it or (2) just pretending you understand?
d) Do you prefer speaking English with a (1) native speaker or (2) non-native speaker?
e) When you meet a native speaker of English, (1) do you usually try to talk to the person or (2) are you too shy to say anything?
f) When you are reading and see a word you don't know, do you usually (1) try to guess its meaning or (2) look it up in the dictionary?
g) When you use English and make mistakes, does it bother you (1) a lot or (2) only a little?

2 *Pair work* Now compare answers.

3 *Group work* What are the five most useful things you can do to improve your English? Talk about the things above and other ideas of your own.

Drawing by Richter; © 1989 The New Yorker Magazine, Inc.

7 Don't drink the water!

1 SNAPSHOT

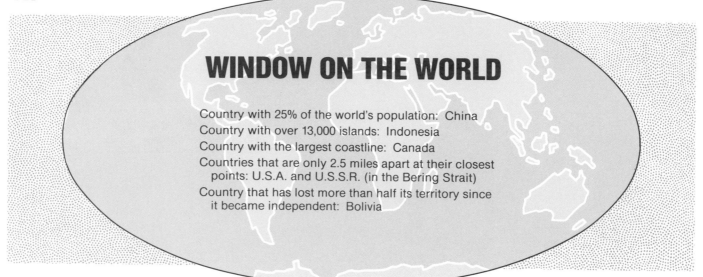

WINDOW ON THE WORLD

Country with 25% of the world's population: China

Country with over 13,000 islands: Indonesia

Country with the largest coastline: Canada

Countries that are only 2.5 miles apart at their closest
points: U.S.A. and U.S.S.R. (in the Bering Strait)

Country that has lost more than half its territory since
it became independent: Bolivia

Discussion

Can you give one more fact about each of the countries above?

What are some interesting facts about your country?

2 CONVERSATION 📼

São Paulo

Salvador (Bahia)

1 Listen.

A: I'm thinking of going to Brazil next year, Maria.

B: Oh, great! I'm sure you'll have a good time.

A: What places do tourists visit in Brazil?

B: Well, a lot of people go to Rio for Carnival. And nowadays, lots of people are visiting the Amazon to take river trips.

A: Oh, really? That sounds interesting. And when's a good time to visit?

B: Well, I like Rio in the spring or fall because it's not too hot then.

2 Listen to the rest of the conversation. What does Maria say about these cities in Brazil: Brasília, São Paulo, and Salvador (Bahia)?

3 *Pair work* A visitor wants information about your country. What places do tourists like to visit? Why? Role-play a conversation like the one above.

3 PRONUNCIATION: Consonant clusters with /s/

1 Listen and practice these words.

Consonant + /s/		/s/ + consonant		/s/ + consonant + /s/	
likes	trips	just	east	coasts	consists
visits	facts	cost	west	dentists	tourists

2 *Pair work* Listen to these questions. Take turns asking and answering them.

Which coast of the United States is Boston on, the east or the west?
What are the most interesting sights for tourists around here?

4 GRAMMAR FOCUS: Adverbials of purpose and reason

Venezuela, South America

> Many people go to Brazil **to visit Rio.**
> **for Carnival.**
> **on business.**
>
> Tourists like to go to Europe **because they want to see the museums.**
> **so they can visit castles and cathedrals.**
>
> Some people don't go in the summer **because it's too hot.**
> **because of the humidity.**

1 *Pair work* Complete these phrases using adverbials.

a) Nowadays many tourists like to visit Australia ...
b) Most people don't like to go to Alaska in the winter ...
c) Not many tourists visit Antarctica yet ...
d) People love to visit Paris ...
e) More and more people travel to South America these days ...

2 Now make statements about five other places.

Alaska

5 WORD POWER: See for yourself

1 *Pair work* Look at these phrases about countries and arrange them into four categories: (a) good points, (b) problems, (c) sightseeing, and (d) transportation. Some phrases have more than one category.

.... exciting cities
.... high crime rate
.... beautiful scenery
.... friendly people
.... fantastic museums
.... too many tourists

.... excellent trains
.... terrible poverty
.... reasonable hotels
.... safe at night
.... poor roads
.... good prices

2 Think of a country or city you know well. How many phrases can you think of to describe its good and bad points?

6 AROUND THE WORLD

1 *Group work* Choose a country to talk about and discuss these questions. One student takes notes.

Why do people like to visit it?
What do they like to do and see?
Is there anything people don't like about it?

2 *Class activity* Groups report to the class and answer any questions.

7 DIFFERENT CUSTOMS

1 Read this information.

Brazil Never go out with your hair wet.
Canada and the United States Don't arrive early if you are
    invited to someone's home.
Indonesia Never point to anything with your foot.
Japan Take off your shoes before you enter someone's home.
Muslim countries Don't eat with your left hand.
Samoa Don't eat when you are walking in public.
Thailand Never touch a child on the head.

2 *Group work* What other interesting customs do you know?
What customs should visitors to your country know about?

8 CONVERSATION 🔲

1 Listen.

A: Guess what! I just got invited to my teacher's house for
    dinner!
B: Oh, that's nice.
A: Yeah, but what do you do when you're invited to
    someone's home here?
B: Oh, you usually bring a small gift.
A: Really? Like what?
B: Well, some flowers or a bottle of wine.
A: OK. And is it all right to bring a friend along?
B: Well, if you want to bring someone, you should call
    first and ask if it's OK.

2 *Discussion* Do you usually bring a gift when you are
invited to someone's home? If so, what kind of gift? Is it
all right to bring a friend?

3 *Role play* Have a conversation like the one above.
Use your own information.

9 GRAMMAR FOCUS: Clauses with *when* and *if* 📼

When you're invited to someone's home for dinner, you should bring something.
you usually bring a gift.
you shouldn't arrive early.

If you go out to dinner with friends, you usually share the bill.
you always leave a tip.
you should be on time.

1 Complete these sentences with information about your country or a country you know. Then compare with a partner.

a) In . . . , if people invite you to their home, . . .
b) If you go out with friends for dinner, . . .
c) When a friend gets engaged, . . .
d) When you are introduced to someone for the first time, . . .
e) When a friend has a birthday, . . .
f) If a friend is in the hospital, . . .
g) When someone is going to have a baby, . . .

2 Now write three statements about customs in your country.
Then compare with a partner.

10 LISTENING 📼

1 *Pair work* Think of three things that make life easy and three things that make life difficult for a person living in a foreign country.

2 Listen to a radio broadcast by a foreign journalist in Japan talking about some of his experiences there.

What does he think is the most difficult
thing about learning a foreign
language?
Why is he able to read more books in
Japan?
What other advantages does he mention?

3 *Class activity* Have you had similar experiences? What is the most difficult thing about learning a foreign language for you?

11 WHAT'S YOUR ADVICE?

1 *Role play*

Student A

You are visiting your partner's country and you want some advice. Ask these questions and other questions of your own.

If I visit a church/temple/mosque, what should I do?
What happens if I get invited to stay in someone's home?
Do people mind if you take pictures of them?
I'd like to visit the countryside. Where's a good place to go?
When someone invites you out, who pays?

Student B

You are talking to someone who is visiting your country. Answer his or her questions and give as much information as you can.

2 Now change partners and roles and do the role play again.

Useful expressions

The most important thing
  is . . . For example, . . .
One thing to remember is . . .
Well, that depends . . .

12 WRITING: Before you go . . .

1 What should a visitor to your country know? Think about points like these and make notes.

dressing appropriately   taking photographs
staying as a house guest or in hotels   meeting people
traveling by bus or train   eating out
giving and receiving gifts   shopping

2 Now choose five points and write a composition.

When you visit my country, there are some important things you should know.

3 *Group work* Take turns reading each other's compositions. Ask and answer questions about the compositions.

> ▶Interchange 7:
> Studying abroad
> Would you make a good student advisor? Turn to page 109 and find out.

13 READING: Culture check

Read these statements about cultural behavior. Is it the same or different in your country? Write **Y** (yes) if it is the same or **N** (no) if it is different. Then compare your answers with a partner.

1 People often kiss friends on the cheek when they meet.
2 People usually shake hands when they are introduced to someone.
3 It's OK to blow your nose in public.
4 It's all right to chew gum while talking to someone.
5 It's OK to ask people how much they earn.
6 It's all right to ask someone what his or her religion is.
7 It's common to bargain when you buy things in stores or shops.
8 It's common to introduce yourself to new neighbors and give them a small gift.
9 In an office, people usually prefer to be called by their first name.
10 In high schools, it's common to call a teacher by his or her first name.
11 Students always stand up when the teacher enters the classroom.
12 People always arrive on time when they are invited to someone's house.
13 It's OK to drop by a friend's house without calling first.
14 If you are with strangers and want to smoke, you should always ask if it's OK.
15 You should take a small gift when you're invited to someone's house for dinner.
16 It's OK to bring a friend or family member when you're invited to a party at someone's home.
17 It's OK to ask for a second helping when eating at a friend's house.
18 When friends eat out together, each person usually pays his or her share of the bill.
19 Parents usually decide who their children will marry.
20 Teenagers go out on dates a lot.
21 A man usually gives a woman a gift when they go out on a date.
22 Young people usually live with their parents after they get married.

To see how an American or Canadian would usually respond to this culture check, see page 132.

8 Getting things done

1 SNAPSHOT

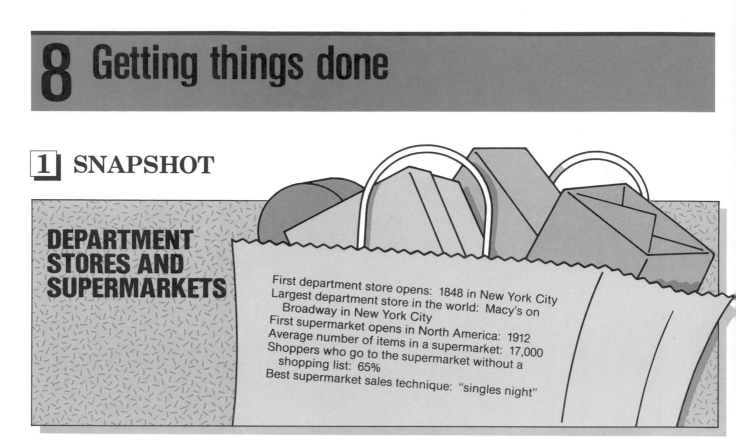

DEPARTMENT STORES AND SUPERMARKETS

First department store opens: 1848 in New York City
Largest department store in the world: Macy's on Broadway in New York City
First supermarket opens in North America: 1912
Average number of items in a supermarket: 17,000
Shoppers who go to the supermarket without a shopping list: 65%
Best supermarket sales technique: "singles night"

Discussion

What is your favorite supermarket? Your favorite department store? Why?

What are three things in your local supermarket that are probably not sold in other countries?

What special sales techniques do supermarkets and department stores have in your city?

2 WORD POWER: Consumer affairs

1 *Pair work* Match these places and activities.
Then think of two more things you can do in each place.

a) in a supermarket
b) in an electronics store
c) at a photocopy center
d) on an airplane
e) in a bank

.... buy frozen food
.... have lunch
.... get cash from a machine
.... get a stereo fixed
.... send a fax
.... get passport photos
.... make photocopies
.... make a phone call
.... see a movie
.... listen to music
.... use a restroom

2 *Group work* What kinds of things can you do in these places?

a department store   a post office   an amusement park

48

3 CONVERSATION 🔊

1 Listen.

A: Do you know where I can get a passport photo taken around here?
B: Well, I think there's a place on Center Street downtown.
A: Oh. Do you know any place closer?
B: Let me think. Oh! There's a place in the shopping center where you can get one taken for five dollars.
A: OK, that's great. Thanks!

2 *Role play* Ask where you can do these things.

buy some stamps   buy a birthday card   get a good haircut

---

4 GRAMMAR FOCUS: *Get* and *have* + participle 🔊

Do you know where I could **get a passport photo taken?**	You can could	**get one taken** downtown.
Can you tell me where I could **have film developed?**	You can could	**have it developed** at Fotomat.

1 Complete these conversations with *get* or *have* + participle. Then check with a partner.

A: Oh no! It's stopped again! Do you know where I can .... (watch / repair)?
B: Sure. You can .... at the Time Shop on Second Street.

A: My car isn't running right. Can you tell me where I could .... (it / service)?
B: Yeah, you can .... at Shelly's Service Center downtown.

A: I need some photocopies. Can you tell me where I can .... (color photocopies / make)?
B: Well, you could .... at Shaw's. They have a new photocopier that can do that.

A: Oh, the heel just came off my shoe! Do you know where I could .... (it / repair)?
B: Sure. You can .... just two blocks down this street. There's a shoe repair shop on the corner.

2 *Pair work* Take turns. Student A asks the questions above. Student B gives real information.

3 Now ask questions about three things *you* want to have done.

5 PRONUNCIATION: Consonant contrast /s/ and /ʃ/ 📼

1 Listen to the difference between these words. Then practice them.

With /s/: seat   sign   Sue   suit   gas   mess   class

With /ʃ/: sheet   shine   shoe   shoot   gash   mesh   clash

2 Listen to eight more words. Do you hear a word with /s/ or /ʃ/? Write 1 for /s/ and 2 for /ʃ/.

3 Now look at the conversations in Exercise 4 again and circle the sounds /s/ and /ʃ/. Then practice the conversations with a partner.

6 LISTENING 📼

Listen to two people talking about Brazil and France. Take notes.

What interesting things can you see and do on the streets in both countries?

7 DIFFERENT PLACES, DIFFERENT WAYS!

Group work   Talk about things you can have done in your city or country. Use the cues below.

Can you . . .

have meals delivered to your home?
get a suit or dress made in a department store?
get free medical advice over the telephone?
do grocery shopping 24 hours a day?
get shoes shined in a bus or train station?
buy a hot meal from a street vendor?
have groceries delivered to your home?
get your blood pressure checked in a shopping mall?
have shoes repaired on the street?
have milk or eggs delivered to your door?

A: Can you have meals delivered to your home here?
B: Well, you can have pizza or even Chinese food delivered from some restaurants. You have to check in the phone book. Usually you can't have French food delivered.
C: Giovanni, in Italy, can you have meals delivered to your home?
D: . . .

8 CONVERSATION 📼

1 Listen.

A: I've got a friend coming for the weekend who loves jazz. Where's a good place to take her?

B: Uh, why not take her to the New Orleans Club? That's a great place to hear live music.

C: Yeah, but it's hard to get in on the weekend. I like the Back Door better because it's not so crowded.

A: Oh, yeah? Do they have dancing there?

C: Uh, I don't think so.

2 *Discussion*

Where is an interesting place to take a visitor in your city or town?
Is there a good place to hear live music?
Can you recommend a popular place for dancing?

3 *Role play* Close your books and have a conversation like the one above. Use your own information.

9 GRAMMAR FOCUS: Nouns with infinitives; clauses with *because* 📼

Where's a good **place to hear live music?**	I like the New Orleans Club **because they have terrific music.**
When's a good **time to go?**	Weekdays are best **because it's not so crowded then.**

Complete these sentences with information about your city or town. Then compare with a partner.

a) The best place to get coffee near here is . . . because . . .

b) My favorite place to go for a snack after class is . . . because . . .

c) A good store to find books in English is . . . because . . .

d) A great place to buy interesting gifts is . . . because . . .

Drawing by Ziegler;
© *1989 The New Yorker Magazine, Inc.*

51

10 FREE FUN

1 *Group work* What interesting things can you do in your town or city that don't cost anything? When is the best time to do these things? Take turns giving your suggestions.

A: One thing I love to do during the spring is to have a picnic in the park. It's really nice then because . . .

B: A great thing to do on hot evenings is to walk along the canal. It doesn't cost anything, and it's fun because . . .

2 *Class activity* Compare your suggestions.

11 LISTENING

1 Listen to Nancy, Charlie, and Marsha talking about three different places and take notes. What kinds of places are they describing (for example, a bank, a disco)?

2 Listen again. Why do they like or dislike each place?

> ▶ **Interchange 8:**
> **Do you have a minute?**
> What does your city have to offer? Turn to page 110.

12 WRITING: Recommendations

A friend from overseas is planning to visit your city (or town) for the first time and wants to know about the things below. Write a letter giving your suggestions and reasons for where to go.

learn about local history
see interesting architecture
watch people making handicrafts

go to theater performances
hear live musicians play
buy interesting souvenirs

Dear Tina,
I'm glad to hear you're coming for a visit! It will be good to see you again. Here are some suggestions for the things you asked about. A good place to learn about local history is . . . because . . .

San Antonio, Texas

13 READING: Favorites

1 Read these descriptions of interesting places and events. What do you think the writer likes best about each one?

A great place to shop

I love shopping in Tokyo. And one of my favorite stores there is Parco. Well, it's actually four stores in one. Parco is very popular with young people. You feel middle aged there if you're over 30! Parco is known for its incredible window displays and fascinating boutiques. It even has its own theaters: you can see a movie or a play when you need a break from shopping. And what I like most is that no one bothers you. You can wander around as much as you like.

A wild week

One of the most interesting events in the U.S. is the Mardi Gras in New Orleans. It's a week when people go crazy. The great thing is that there's something different to do and see every day. There are parades, luncheons, pageants, and about ninety carnival balls. And when you get tired of the carnival, you can listen to all kinds of music, from Fats Domino to Andy Gibb, as well as some of New Orleans' famous jazz musicians.

More than the menu

The restaurant I enjoy the most when I'm in London is the Grill Room in the Savoy. It has excellent British as well as French food. It's a very elegant place, and it's always full of interesting people, which is why I like to go there. You're sure to see a duke or duchess, a well-known politician or TV personality, or a beautiful model or a movie star. The restaurant reminds me of what London must have been like in the 1920s.

A ride you'll never forget

The train ride from Cuzco to Machu Picchu in Peru is one of the most spectacular in the world. It's on a narrow-gauge railway and travels along the crest of the Andes Mountains. The views are unforgettable. Cuzco is very high, about 12,000 feet, and it's an incredible place. It's the center of Inca culture. Throughout the trip, you can see all sorts of interesting people, and then you finally arrive at the Lost City of the Incas.

2 Now answer these questions.

a) What do you think attracts shoppers to Parco?
b) What kind of people would enjoy the Mardi Gras?
c) What is the main reason people go to the Grill Room?
d) What are two things people like about the train ride from Cuzco to Machu Picchu?

9 Is that a fact?

1 SNAPSHOT

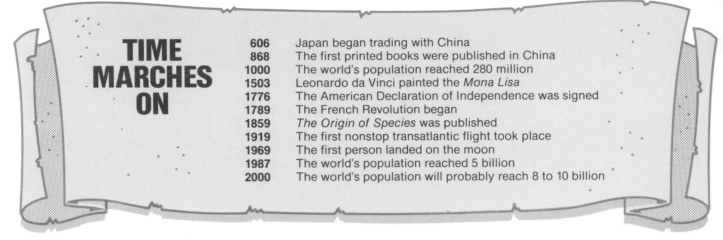

TIME MARCHES ON

606	Japan began trading with China
868	The first printed books were published in China
1000	The world's population reached 280 million
1503	Leonardo da Vinci painted the *Mona Lisa*
1776	The American Declaration of Independence was signed
1789	The French Revolution began
1859	*The Origin of Species* was published
1919	The first nonstop transatlantic flight took place
1969	The first person landed on the moon
1987	The world's population reached 5 billion
2000	The world's population will probably reach 8 to 10 billion

Discussion

Can you add three more famous dates in world history?
Do you know who wrote *The Origin of Species?* Why was it famous?
What are three important events in the history of your country?

2 CONVERSATION

1 *Pair work* How many questions can you answer?

A: Can you help me with this history quiz?
B: I'll try. What do you need to know?
A: Well, first, when did the Berlin Wall start to come down?
B: ....
A: And how long has the United Nations been in existence?
B: ....
A: OK, and how many symphonies did Beethoven compose?
B: ....
A: And when did jazz first become popular?
B: ....
A: Hmm. Now just one more. In what century was Napoleon emperor of France?
B: ....
A: Thanks. Gee, you're great at history.
B: I should be. I'm a history teacher.

2 Listen and check your answers. Then practice the conversation.

The opening of the Berlin Wall

54

③ GRAMMAR FOCUS: Prepositions and adverbs 🔲

When did it happen?	How long has it been like that?
In the 1960s.	**Since** 1950.
During the seventies.	**Since** the nineteenth century.
From 1914 **to** 1918.	**From** 1989 **till** now.
About two hundred years **ago**.	**For** (the past) two hundred years.

1 Complete these conversations using words from the box. Then practice them.

A: When did the *Titanic* sink?
B: I think it was about eighty or ninety years ....

A: When was the first flight in a jumbo jet?
B: I think it was .... 1970.

A: When was John F. Kennedy President of the United States?
B: He was president .... 1961 .... 1963.

A: When did the Beatles first become popular?
B: They first became popular .... the sixties.

A: How long has this statue been a national landmark?
B: This statue has been a national landmark .... about fifty years.

The Titanic

2 *Pair work* Now write six questions like these about past events.

④ HISTORY QUIZ

Group work Take turns asking the questions you wrote in Exercise 3, part 2. Then ask follow-up questions.

A: When was the Russian Revolution?
B: I think it started in 1917.
A: Who was the leader of the revolution?
C: It was Lenin, wasn't it?

Who was...? Where...?
When...?
Why did...? Did...?
How did...? What did...?

⑤ PRONUNCIATION: Syllable stress 🔲

1 Arrange these words into three groups: words with the main stress on the 1st, 2nd, or 3rd syllable.

astronaut	childhood	independent	population
biography	economist	information	president
century	engineer	popular	revolution

2 Now listen and check.

6 WORD POWER: Professions

1 Match each word with a definition. Then compare with a partner.

a) an astronaut
b) a biographer
c) a composer
d) an economist
e) an explorer
f) a psychologist
g) a politician
h) a scientist

.... a person who studies trade, industry, and the management of money
.... someone who writes music
.... a person who does work in physics, chemistry, biology, etc.
.... someone who travels in a spacecraft
.... an author who writes about someone's life
.... someone who travels in order to discover new places
.... a person whose business is to help run a government
.... someone who studies the human mind and its influence on learning and human behavior

Scientist

2 *Pair work* Give definitions for these professions:
an inventor, a journalist, a movie director, a surgeon.

3 *Group work* Can you name a famous person for any four of the professions above? What was each person famous for?

Astronaut

7 LISTENING 🔲

1 Listen to a radio program about the American actor James Dean. Look at these questions and take notes.

When was James Dean born?
Where was he born?
Where did he spend his childhood?
How did he become a movie star?
Why was he so popular?
When did he die, and how?

2 *Pair work* Take turns using your notes to talk about the life of James Dean.

8 WRITING: A biography

Write about someone who achieved something important during his or her life. Include information about these things.

Georgia O'Keeffe (1887–1986)

who the person is
what he or she is famous for
the person's early life
how he or she became famous
later life and achievements
what he or she is remembered for

```
Georgia O'Keeffe was one of the
most famous painters of the
twentieth century.  She was ninety-
eight when she died in 1986.  She
left behind over 900 beautiful
pictures of flowers, landscapes, city
views, shells, stones, bones, and
clouds, which gave a unique picture
of the American landscape.

Georgia O'Keeffe was born in ...
```

9 CONVERSATION 🔲

▶ **Interchange 9: History buff**
Find out how good you are at history. Student A turn to page 111 and Student B to page 112.

1 Listen.

A: I've just been reading an interesting article about robots. Did you know that the typical factory worker in the future will be a robot?
B: Really? That's scary.
A: Yeah, and they'll even use robots to make and repair other robots.
B: That's hard to imagine. And when is this supposed to happen?
A: Within thirty years. And robots will also be building factories in outer space and even mining minerals on the moon.
B: Hey, maybe by then they'll have invented a robot to clean my apartment!

2 *Discussion* What kinds of jobs do you think robots will be doing in the future?

3 Now listen to the rest of the conversation and take notes.

What jobs will be done by robots?
What else will robots be doing in the future?

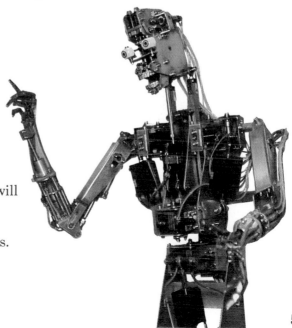

10 GRAMMAR FOCUS: Future 🔲

With *will*	With *going to*
A typical factory worker **will be** a robot.	Many jobs **are going to be** done by robots.
Future continuous	**Future perfect**
Robots **will be building** factories in space.	They **will have found** many uses for robots in the home.

1 Match the information to make sentences. More than one answer may be possible. Then compare with a partner.

A

a) In the future, some cities
b) Scientists believe the world's climate
c) Fifty years from now, motorists
d) By the year 2050, medical researchers
e) Within a hundred years, people

B

.... will be driving solar-powered cars.
.... will have discovered a way to prevent aging.
.... will be living on the moon.
.... will ban all private cars.
.... will have found a cure for the common cold.
.... is going to get warmer in the next fifty years.
.... will be built under the ocean.
.... are only going to work a two-day week.

2 *Pair work* Take turns completing column A with your own information.

3 *Group work*

Which three countries do you think will be the most powerful by 2050?
Which three products in science and technology are going to affect our lives the most in the next twenty years?
What three jobs do you think people won't be doing in fifty years?
What are the three most important changes that will have occurred on Earth by 2050?

11 THINGS WILL BE DIFFERENT!

Group work Talk about these questions.

What do you think you'll be doing a year from now? How about in five years?
Do you think you'll still be living in this town?
What are three things you think you'll have done in the next five years?
What are three things you won't have done?
In what ways do you think you'll have changed?

Now   *Five years from now*

12 READING: Who really discovered America?

Can you think of three facts about Christopher Columbus?
Compare your information with a partner and then read this passage.

For many years, people believed that the Italian explorer Christopher Columbus discovered America. But, in fact, others had reached America before him. Thousands of years ago, Asians crossed the Bering Strait to Alaska and then moved through North America and on to South America. Others have claimed that travelers from Europe and China also visited America. According to some people, sailors from China crossed the Pacific to Mexico in A.D. 459. Irish explorers also may have visited America in the ninth and tenth centuries. Irish people living in Iceland before the Norsemen, who came from Scandinavia, reached it in the ninth century. They may have sailed from Iceland to America after the Norsemen arrived.

The Norsemen themselves may also have visited America. They were used to sailing long distances in their ships. Some Norse stories tell of a Norseman called Bjarni Herjolfsson who visited America in A.D. 986. Another Norseman named Leif Ericsson probably lived for a time in Newfoundland in Canada but then returned to Greenland. However, the first Western explorer we can be sure about was Christopher Columbus. He left Spain on August 3, 1492, and on October 12th, he arrived in the Bahamas. Columbus thought he had arrived in the Indies (the name then used for Asia). That is why he called the people Indians. He spent many weeks sailing around the Caribbean and then went back to Spain. He made several more voyages to the New World, though he never actually landed in North America.

So, who was America named after? It was named after another Italian explorer, Amerigo Vespucci, who was a friend of Columbus's and who later explored the coastline of the New World.

Leif Ericsson

Christopher Columbus

1 Write **T** (true) or **F** (false). For the statements you mark false, give the correct information.

a) The first people to travel to North America came from Europe.
b) Some people believe that travelers from China visited America nearly 1,500 years ago.
c) Columbus landed in North America on October 12, 1492.

2 Now write two more statements like these about the passage. Then ask a classmate if they are true or false.

Review of Units 7-9

1 Special times

1 *Group work* What interesting traditions and customs are there in your country for these events? Choose one event and prepare a three-minute class talk about it.

special holidays   marriage   New Year's   seasons

The Feast of Lanterns is a popular celebration in Korea. It commemorates the birth of Buddha and is held on the eighth day of the fourth lunar month. Elaborate ceremonies are held in Buddhist temples across the entire country, and lanterns are carried in a parade through the city streets.

2 *Class activity* Groups take turns giving their talks and answering any questions.

2 Where to go

1 *Class activity* Go around the class and find out where in your city or town you can do the things below. Ask each question to a different person.

A: Where can you have a fax sent?
B: Well, you can get it sent at . . .   *(or)*
     You could have it sent at . . .

a) have a fax sent
b) get a photocopy made
c) get a document or letter typed
d) have a photo taken
e) have something translated
f) get some legal advice
g) get a visa renewed
h) send money to someone abroad
i) get information on housing
j) buy some used furniture

2 *Pair work* Compare your information.

3 Listening 📼

1 Nancy is planning to travel around Australia. She's talking to David about her trip. What does he tell her about these things? Take notes.

a) interesting places to visit
b) things to do in each place
c) where to stay in each place

2 *Role play* Use your notes and practice the conversation between Nancy and David.

4 How good is your history?

1 Try to answer these questions. Then compare with a partner. (Answers are on page 132.)

a) Can you name a pop group that was famous in the 1970s?
b) Who developed the theory of relativity?
c) When did India gain its independence from Great Britain?
d) Who was Jacqueline Onassis's first husband?
e) What was Sigmund Freud famous for?

2 *Pair work* Now think of five more questions like these. (Make sure you know the answers.)

3 *Group work* Take turns asking your questions. Who has the most correct answers?

5 Famous people

1 *Group work* Choose two famous people from the box below. Give as much information about them as you can. One student takes notes.

Paula Abdul	Jane Fonda	Bruce Lee	Luciano Pavarotti
Corazon Aquino	Martha Graham	Nelson Mandela	Pelé
Simón Bolívar	Mikhail Gorbachev	Marcello Mastroianni	Elvis Presley
Jorge Luis Borges	Julio Iglesias	Melina Mercouri	Gabriela Sabatini
Sonia Braga	Janet Jackson	Midori	Desmond Tutu
Tom Cruise	John F. Kennedy	Marilyn Monroe	Mike Tyson
Catherine Deneuve	Martin Luther King, Jr.	Eddie Murphy	
Gérard Depardieu	Akira Kurosawa	Yoko Ono	

2 *Class activity* Groups compare information. Which group knows the most about each person?

10 There's no place like home

1 SNAPSHOT

AT HOME

North American families that move every year: 25%
Single-person households today: 25%
            30 years ago: 10%
Household chores people hate most:

1 washing dishes	**5** cleaning
2 cleaning bathrooms	**6** vacuuming
3 ironing	**7** washing windows
4 scrubbing floors	**8** cooking

Average distance a homemaker walks every day doing
  household chores: 10 miles (16 kilometers)
Most common causes of accidents around the home:
  bicycles, stairs, doors

Discussion

How often have you moved in the last five years? In your lifetime?
What are the three household chores you hate doing the most?
How much time do you spend every week doing household chores?

2 CONVERSATION 📼

1 Listen.

A: Have you moved to your new apartment yet, Fred?
B: Yes, we moved in last Saturday.
A: So, how do you like it?
B: Oh, it's great! There's plenty of room, and it's quiet, too.
A: Yeah? Uh, what's the building like? Does it have a pool?
B: No, it doesn't have a pool, but there's a patio downstairs and a big yard for the kids to play in.
A: It sounds nice.
B: It is. Why don't you come over this weekend and see it?
A: OK. I'd like to.

2 Now listen to the rest of the conversation and take notes. What does Fred say about the neighborhood?

3 *Role play* Close your books and have a conversation like the one above. Use your own information about the place where you live or a place you would like to move to.

3 GRAMMAR FOCUS: Conjunctions, adverbs, and prepositions 📼

It has a patio, **and** it has a nice yard, **too.**
Besides having a patio, it has a nice yard.

There's plenty of room **as well,** and it's quiet.
In addition to having plenty of room, it's quiet.

It **also** has a big garden.
As well as having a big garden, there's a patio.

It has a nice patio, **but** it doesn't have a pool.
Although there's no pool, there's a nice patio.

There's no balcony; **however,** there's a view.
Even though there's no balcony, there's a view.

1 Complete these sentences using words from the grammar box. More than one correct answer may be possible.

a) .... having a large yard, my apartment building has a pool.
b) .... there is no shopping center near my house, there's a good supermarket down the street.
c) .... having lots of buses, the city has a good subway system.
d) The city has good taxis ...., and they are very cheap.
e) There's no airport in the city; ...., there's one about fifty miles away.

2 Now make six sentences like these about your home and city (or town). Then compare with a partner.

4 LISTENING 📼

1 Kelly is looking for a place to rent. She is talking to an agent. What kind of place is she looking for? Listen and fill in the chart.

2 Now listen to the agent describing a property, and complete the chart.

3 *Pair work* Use the chart and role-play the conversation between Kelly and the agent.

	Client's needs	*Agent's property*
Apartment/ house		
Price		
Number of bedrooms		
Furnished/ unfurnished		
Location		
Special features		

5 HOME SWEET HOME

Pair work Talk about the place where you live.
Ask these and other questions of your own.

Your home

Do you live in a house or an apartment?
How long have you lived there?
How big is it?
Does it have a . . .?
Do you like it there?
Is there anything you don't like about it?

Your neighborhood

What are your neighbors like?
What kind of neighborhood is it?
Do a lot of families with young children live there?
Are there many older people living there?
Are there any shops in the neighborhood?
Is there good transportation nearby?
What do you like most about the neighborhood?
Is there anything you don't like about it?

6 CONVERSATION 📼

1 Listen.

A: Hello?
B: Hello, Ms. Crocker. This is Mr. Roberts.
A: Uh, Mr. Roberts . . . in apartment 205?
B: No, not 205, 305.
A: Oh, yes. What can I do for you? Is it the refrigerator again?
B: No, it's not the refrigerator. It's the oven this time.
A: Oh? Well, what's wrong with it?
B: Well, I think something's wrong with the temperature control. Everything I try to cook gets burned.
A: Really? OK, I'll get someone to look at it right away.
B: Thanks a lot.
A: Uh, by the way, Mr. Roberts, are you sure it's the oven and not your cooking?

2 *Pair work* Now close your books and have a conversation like the one above. Think of something to complain about in your home.

7 PRONUNCIATION: Contrastive stress 📟

1 When we contrast two words, we stress the word we are contrasting.
Listen and practice.

A: Are you calling about the bedroom fan?
B: No, the **kitchen** fan.

A: Are you calling about the bedroom window?
B: No, the bedroom **door.**

2 Mark the words that have contrastive stress in the sentences below.
Listen and check. Then practice the sentences.

a) A: Did you ask for two light bulbs?
   B: No, I asked for three.

b) A: Do you need a new telephone?
   B: No, a new television.

c) A: Is it the hot water faucet that leaks?
   B: No, it's the cold one.

---

8 WORD POWER: Appliances

1 Find suitable sentences that describe a problem with each of these
appliances. Then compare with a partner.

a) air conditioner .... It's too cold; it freezes everything.
b) central heating .... It gets too hot and burns clothes.
c) faucet .... No water comes out.
d) iron .... The bulb needs to be replaced.
e) lamp .... It's not cooling properly.
f) refrigerator .... The picture isn't clear.
g) stove .... One of the burners doesn't work.
h) telephone .... It's not heating right.
i) television .... I can't get a dial tone.

2 *Pair work*   Now describe other things that can go wrong with some
of the appliances above. Then compare your suggestions around the class.

---

9 LISTENING 📟

Listen to three tenants complaining to their
building manager, and complete the chart.

	Tenant's complaint	Manager's response
#1		
#2		
#3		

10 WHAT'S THE PROBLEM?

Role play

Student A: Tenant

You have just moved to a new apartment. There are several things wrong with it, and you are not happy about them. Phone the manager and complain about the problems.

Student B: Apartment manager

A new tenant phones you. Listen to his or her complaints and say what you will do. Use some of these expressions.

Asking for more information	*Offering to do something*
What seems to be the matter?	I'll fix it today.
What's wrong with it?	I'll check on it tomorrow.
Can you tell me what the problem is?	OK. I'll come by and have a look at it.

11 WRITING: Letters of complaint

1 Choose one of these situations and write a letter describing the problems and what needs to be done.

There are several things that need fixing in your apartment, but the owner lives in a different city.

There are many problems and improvements needed in your neighborhood.

Dear Mr. Jones,
   I'm a tenant in apartment ... I'd like to point out a few things that need fixing in the apartment.
   First, in the kitchen...

Dear City Council:

I live here on ... Street in ...   I enjoy living here; however, there are a number of problems in the neighborhood that need your attention.

First, the street lights ...

2 *Class activity* Put your letters on the bulletin board. Who has the most unusual problem?

12 READING: Marking territory

What kinds of pictures, objects, and personal items do you keep in your office, study, or bedroom to show that it is yours?

Why do you think it is important to mark personal territory?

How do home owners personalize their houses?

▶ Interchange 10:
You sold me a piece of junk!
Find out if the customer is always right. Student A turn to page 111 and Student B to page 112.

Now read this article and answer the questions below.

In everyday language, we talk of "my place," "our home," and "their neighborhood." We think of our home as our own private territory. People need a place of their own, where they can get away from others and feel a sense of being in charge. Even within families, we attach ourselves to personal territories; for example, the kitchen tends to "belong" to the one who prepares the meals. We like to have our own workrooms and our own bedrooms, or at least our own side of the bed! People personalize their territories to emphasize where one ends and another begins.

Within the home, territorial boundaries depend on the level of intimacy of different rooms and spaces. On the doorstep and in the front hallway, we meet strangers and people making deliveries. Friends and relatives are invited into the living room or kitchen, but rarely are people from outside the immediate family admitted to an adult's bedroom. (See the chart at right.)

Personalizing our territories shows how attached we feel to them. A study of American university dormitories showed how personalization of students' spaces was related to their sense of belonging to the university as a whole. The investigators counted the number of personal items in the students' rooms, such as posters, stereos, and rugs, and found that the students who dropped out had the least number of personal items on display.

The same thing is true of neighborhoods. Look around you in your own neighborhood. Look at the houses or apartments that show personalization: new fences and boundary markers, door colors that stand out from the rest, or freshly painted window frames. Noting how territories are marked should allow you to predict who is most likely to stay and become involved in the community.

When getting established in a new town or country, uprooted people are likely to put up pictures of their old home. The greater the number of local objects they put on display, however, the more likely they are to stay and form relationships in their new community.

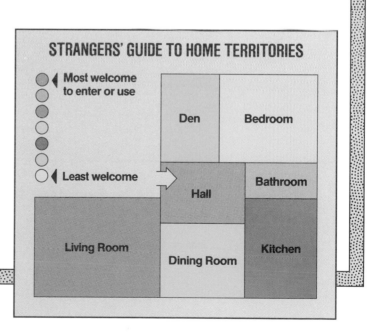

STRANGERS' GUIDE TO HOME TERRITORIES

◀ Most welcome to enter or use

◀ Least welcome

Den | Bedroom

Hall | Bathroom

Living Room | Dining Room | Kitchen

a) Is the information above the same in your family and neighborhood? If not, what are the differences?

b) Are there any items in your classroom or school that show that these places have been personalized?

67

11 What a world we live in!

1 CONVERSATION 🔊

1 Listen.

A: Did you hear that Jerry lost his job?

B: Oh, he did? Gee, that's too bad.

A: Yeah, the company wasn't making money, so they had to lay off some employees.

B: So what's Jerry going to do now?

A: Well, he's thinking of starting his own business.

B: Oh, that's great. I don't know what I'd do if I lost my job. Maybe I'd go back to school. What would you do?

A: Well, first I think I'd probably take a vacation. After that, I guess I'd try working for myself, too.

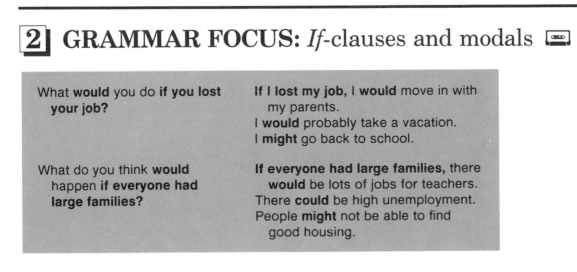

2 *Pair work* Choose one of these questions and discuss it.

What would you do if you lost your job?
What would you do if you wanted to find a good job?

2 GRAMMAR FOCUS: *If*-clauses and modals 🔊

What **would** you do **if you lost your job?**	**If I lost my job, I would** move in with my parents. **I would** probably take a vacation. **I might** go back to school.
What do you think **would** happen **if everyone had large families?**	**If everyone had large families,** there **would** be lots of jobs for teachers. There **could** be high unemployment. People **might** not be able to find good housing.

68

1 Look at these answers. What are the questions?

a) If visitors from outer space landed on Earth, I think they would probably be arrested and put in jail.

b) If cars were banned, there would be much less pollution in the cities.

c) If I had 24 hours to spend $10,000, I'd buy a first-class ticket for a trip around the world.

d) If people only worked a three-day week, they might get just as much work done.

e) If I became the leader of my country, I would make my birthday a national holiday.

f) If someone asked me for a loan, I would say I don't usually lend money.

2 *Pair work* Now take turns asking the questions you wrote above. Give your own answers.

3 Write four more questions with *if*-clauses and take turns asking them around the class.

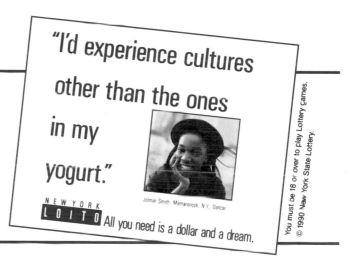

"I'd experience cultures other than the ones in my yogurt."

Jolmar Smith Mamaroneck, N.Y. Dancer

NEW YORK
LOTTO All you need is a dollar and a dream.

You must be 18 or over to play Lottery games.
© 1990 New York State Lottery.

---

3 **LISTENING** 🔊

1 Linda, Robert, and Scott are talking about the lottery. What would they do if they won $10 million? Listen and take notes.

2 What would you do if you won $10 million?

---

4 **PRONUNCIATION:** Plural *s* 🔊

1 Plural *s* can be pronounced /z/, /s/, and /iz/. Put these words into three lists according to the sound of the -*s* ending:

buildings	families	licenses	parents	prisons	streets	weeks
cigarettes	houses	noises	pets	schools	taxes	

2 Listen and check. Then practice the words.

3 Listen and practice these sentences. Pay attention to plural *s*.

Families in apartments shouldn't keep pets such as dogs and cats.

Drivers who have cars with large engines should pay higher taxes.

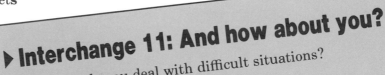

▶ **Interchange 11: And how about you?**

How well do you deal with difficult situations? Find out on page 113.

5 SNAPSHOT

POLLUTION

Most common form of water pollution: soil, sand,
and minerals washed from the land into the water

Amount of water the average North American family
uses per day: 160 gallons

Biggest cause of air pollution in cities (85%): cars,
trucks, and buses

Amount of garbage produced in the U.S. per
year: 144 million tons

Amount of garbage thrown away by the average
North American per day: 6 pounds (2.7 kilograms)

Expected lifespan of a plastic container buried in
the ground: 50,000 years

Discussion

What are the main sources of pollution in your city or country?

How is garbage disposal handled in your country?

What are two reasons for and two against using plastic containers?

6 LISTENING

1 Listen to Helen and Toshi discussing stories in the newspaper.

What are they talking about?
What do they think about each topic?

Do they agree or disagree?

Topic	Helen's opinion	Toshi's opinion
a)		
b)		
c)		

2 *Pair work*   What do you think about the topics above?

7 GRAMMAR FOCUS: Phrases with gerunds 🔲

> **Keeping drugs off the streets** is a real problem.
> **Providing jobs for young people** is our biggest challenge.
> What do you think about **lowering the speed limit?**
>
> A real problem is **keeping drugs off the streets.**
> Our biggest challenge is **providing jobs for young people.**
> **Lowering the speed limit** is not a good idea.

1 Match information in columns A and B to make sentences. Then compare with a partner.

A

a) One of the biggest economic problems
b) Paying for their children's education
c) A problem for many high school graduates
d) An urgent need in many industrial cities
e) Reducing traffic noise
f) Controlling the world's population
g) Banning smoking in public places

B

.... is a concern for people who live near freeways.
.... is keeping inflation down.
.... is reducing air pollution.
.... is one of the greatest challenges we face today.
.... is a problem for many parents.
.... is finding a job.
.... is a good way to protect people's health.

2 Now use your own information to complete the phrases in column A. Then compare with a partner.

8 WORD POWER: World problems

1 *Pair work* Look at this list of world problems. Choose six that are problems in your city, town, or country. Then rank them from 1 to 6.

corruption
crime
drugs
inflation
medical costs
noise
pollution
poverty
public housing
traffic
unemployment
vandalism

2 *Group work* Compare your lists.
What can we do about some of these problems?

3 What are three other problems in your country?

9 IN MY OPINION . . .

1 *Group work*   Take turns discussing the topics below.

A: What do you think about . . . ?
B: Oh, I think it's a good idea because . . .
C: Yeah, I agree. We should . . .
D: Well, I don't think it's necessary because . . .

giving students financial rewards
   when they get high grades
banning cigarette advertising
making companies recycle all
   their waste
getting car owners to pay more
   taxes for public transportation
eliminating all private schools
paying teachers more when their
   students get high test scores
allowing workers to set flexible
   hours

Useful expressions

That's a good point.
Yes, I agree with you.
That's true, but . . .
Maybe you're right, but . . .
Well, I disagree because . . .
Mmm, I think . . .

2 Now think of three other controversial topics.
What does the rest of the class think?

10 WRITING

1 Choose a topic you feel strongly about.
Write a composition giving your reasons.

> I think forcing car owners to pay more taxes for
> public transportation is a good idea. I feel that
> it is important for several reasons...

Use these words and phrases to connect your ideas.

First,	Also . . .
Another thing . . .	In addition,

2 *Pair work*   Exchange compositions. Does your partner agree or
disagree with your opinion? Why?

11 READING: Waste not, want not

Is garbage disposal a problem in your city?
How many different forms of garbage disposal are used?

Disposing of the garbage we produce every day is a major problem in cities around the world. In the United States, over 160 million tons of garbage are produced every year. Ten percent is recycled, ten percent is burned, and the rest is put in landfills. But finding land for new landfills is becoming more difficult.

A city that has solved this problem in an unusual way is Machida, in Tokyo, Japan. They have developed a totally new approach to garbage disposal. The key to the operation is public cooperation. Families must divide their garbage into six categories:

1 garbage that can be easily burned (that is, combustible garbage), such as kitchen and garden trash
2 noncombustible garbage, such as small electrical appliances, plastic tools, and plastic toys
3 products that are poisonous or that cause pollution, such as batteries and fluorescent lights
4 bottles and glass containers that can be recycled
5 metal containers that can be recycled
6 large items, such as furniture and bicycles

The items in categories 1 to 5 are collected on different days. (Large items are only collected upon request.) Then the garbage is taken to a center that looks like a clean new office building or hospital. Inside the center, special equipment is used to sort and process the garbage. Almost everything can be reused: garden or kitchen trash becomes fertilizer; combustible garbage is burned to produce electricity; metal containers and bottles are recycled; and old furniture, clothing, and other useful items are cleaned, repaired, and resold cheaply or given away. The work provides employment for handicapped persons and gives them a chance to learn new skills.

Nowadays, officials from cities around the world visit Machida to see whether they can use some of these ideas and techniques to solve their own garbage disposal problems.

a) Which of the six categories above would these items be placed in?

.... old newspapers   .... soda and beer cans   .... old chinaware (for example,
.... a bed   .... acids and chemicals   plates, cups)

b) In the garbage disposal center, what happens to these things?

a carpet   an old color TV
car tires   old food and vegetables (for example, from supermarkets)

12 How does it work?

1 SNAPSHOT

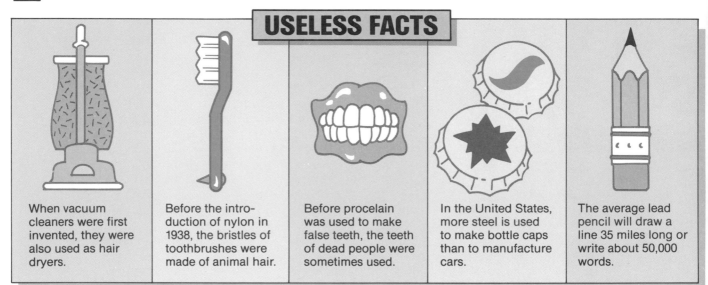

USELESS FACTS

When vacuum cleaners were first invented, they were also used as hair dryers.

Before the introduction of nylon in 1938, the bristles of toothbrushes were made of animal hair.

Before procelain was used to make false teeth, the teeth of dead people were sometimes used.

In the United States, more steel is used to make bottle caps than to manufacture cars.

The average lead pencil will draw a line 35 miles long or write about 50,000 words.

Discussion
What other things are made of porcelain?
What are some other common uses of steel?
Can you add three more "useless" facts to the list above?

2 CONVERSATION

1 Listen.

A: Are you good at crossword puzzles?
B: Well, sometimes.
A: OK. What's this? It's a small piece of curved wire that's used for holding sheets of paper together.
B: Gee, I have no idea.
A: All right. Then how about this one? This instrument, which is usually made of metal or plastic, is used for eating food. It has a handle at one end and two or more points at the other.
B: I'm sorry. I can't guess that one either.

2 Do you know the answers? Check with a partner.

3 *Pair work* Now listen to descriptions of two more things. Can you guess what they are? (Answers are on page 134.)

3 GRAMMAR FOCUS: Relative clauses 🔲

Defining clauses with *that*	Non-defining clauses with *which*
It's a piece of wire. It's used for holding paper together. It's a piece of wire **that's used for holding paper together.**	This thing is used for eating food. It's usually made of metal or plastic. This thing, **which is usually made of metal or plastic,** is used for eating food.

Rewrite these sentences with *that* or *which*.
Then compare with a partner.

a) This is a kitchen appliance. It's used for washing dishes.
b) This appliance has a ten-year guarantee. It's made in Germany.
c) It has a switch. It controls the temperature.
d) The camera has a cover. It's made of leather.
e) This microwave oven fits above the stove. It's the latest model.
f) It's a simple gadget. It has only two parts.
g) This CD player weighs only five ounces. It's portable.
h) The calculator has forty functions. It's made by Sony.
i) It's a pocket-size camera. It uses tiny floppy disks instead of film.
j) The battery compartment holds two batteries. It's at the back of the cassette player.

4 WORD POWER: Definitions

1 *Pair work*   Use the words and phrases in the boxes to give definitions for these words.

a broom	a piggy bank
a bucket	a saw
a corkscrew	a vacuum cleaner
an envelope	wax
glue	a wok

appliance	stuff	carry liquids	open bottles
container	thing	clean carpets	polish things
gadget	tool	cook food	send letters in
machine	utensil	cut wood	stick things together
something		save money in	sweep floors

A: What's a broom?
B: It's a thing that's used for sweeping floors.

A: What's glue?
B: It's stuff that's used to stick things together.

2 Now take turns giving definitions for these things:

a box   a hammer   tape
a calculator   string   a toaster

3 *Group work* Take turns asking for the names of some of the
things you talked about.

A: What's the stuff that's used to stick things together?
B: Oh, I think you mean glue.

---

5 | LISTENING 📼

Listen to a salesperson describing a new product to a customer, and take notes.

What is it?   What features does it have?

---

6 | IT'S HANDY!

1 *Group work* Choose one of these things to talk about.

What's this?
  It's a thing that's used for . . .
  I think it's called a . . .

Can you describe it?
  Yes, it consists of . . .
  I think it has . . .

How does it work? How do you use it?
  Well, first, you . . .

2 Now think of something to describe to
the class. Make notes about it but don't
include its name. Your classmates will
guess what it is.

3 *Class activity* Each group reads its
description. Can anyone guess what it is?

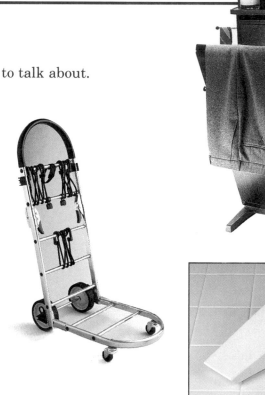

---

7 | PRONUNCIATION: Stress in compound nouns 📼

1 In compound nouns (noun + noun), the first noun receives greater
stress. Listen and practice.

cassette player   **hair** dryer   **rice** cooker   **tooth**brush
coffee machine   **paper** clip   **swimming** pool   **vacuum** cleaner

2 *Pair work* Think of five other compound nouns.
Then read some of them to the class.

8 CONVERSATION 🔲

1 Listen.

A: Gosh, these bonsai trees are really beautiful! How are they grown?

B: Well, first you take a healthy young tree. Almost any kind of tree can be used.

A: Oh, really?

B: Yes. Then some of the leaves and branches are removed. You also have to cut back some of the roots.

A: Why's that?

B: It makes it grow more slowly. Then it's planted in a pot with a little soil.

A: And how do you get it to grow into an interesting shape?

B: Well, wire is used to tie the branches into the shape you want. Later on, when the tree is older, the wire is removed.

A: I see.

B: The tree has to be given plenty of fertilizer. As it grows, it's trimmed to stop it from growing too big. And from time to time, it's taken out of the pot and the roots are cut.

A: Oh, that's very interesting. Thank you.

2 *Pair work*   Now close your books. Can you remember how a bonsai tree is grown?

▶**Interchange 12: Same or different?**

Find out if you have an eye for details. Student A turn to page 114, and Student B to page 116.

9 GRAMMAR FOCUS: The passive 🔲

How **is** it **done?**	The tree **is planted** in a pot. Almost any kind of tree can **be used.**
How **are** they **grown?**	They have to **be given** fertilizer. Some of the leaves **are removed.**

Complete the sentences using *is* or *are* and the correct form of the verbs given.

How paper is made

a) Paper .... usually .... (make) from wood.

b) First, the wood .... (take) to a paper mill.

c) The wood .... then .... (place) in a machine that cuts it into small chips.

d) Next, the chips .... (mix) with water and acid, and then they .... (heat).

e) A thick pulp .... (produce) and chemicals .... (add) to whiten it.

f) Now, it .... (pass) through another machine to flatten it.

g) Heavy steel rollers .... (use) to produce sheets of wet paper.

h) These sheets .... then .... (dry) and .... (press) again to produce paper.

10 STEP BY STEP

1 *Group work* Look at these topics. How many stages can you think
of between the first and last parts in each process?

Sending a letter

First, the letter is written. . . .

Finally, the letter is delivered to the
    person's mailbox.

Making a cup of tea

First, some water is boiled. . . .

Finally, the tea is poured from the teapot
    into the cup.

2 *Class activity* Compare your answers.
Who has the most stages?

11 LISTENING 📼

Listen to the manager at Burger Palace
explaining how Whopping Burgers are
made. Take notes. Then compare your
information with a partner.

12 WRITING

1 Write about how your favorite food is made (or about another topic of
your choice). Describe the different stages in the process.

2 *Pair work* Now read each other's compositions. Can you add any
stages in the process?

13 READING: Advertisements

1 Read these ads for unusual new products. Which products would appeal to someone who . . .

wants to be able to keep in shape at home?
travels abroad a lot?
likes to entertain party guests?
is concerned about his or her health?
doesn't have much time in the morning?

Lap of Luxury

You can swim laps in this 12 by 6 by 4 foot exercise swimming pool because the SwimEx minipool works like a treadmill. The adjustable water current lets you swim in place – and at a pace that's right for your exercise needs.   *Price: $19,950*

Beans to Brew

Sanyo's *Cafe San* is the only 10-cup coffee maker with a coffee grinder built in. So you get freshly ground coffee every time. Just pour in whole beans, set the timer, and a perfect pot of coffee will be waiting for you tomorrow morning.
Price: $189

Talk Is Chip

With most electronic translators, you have to type in the word you want to translate, but not with the VOICE computer *Explorer*. Just speak a word or phrase of English into the VOICE *Explorer* and it will translate the word or phrase into a foreign language and say it aloud.   *Price: $2,000*

Star Search

Now you and your guests can sing like pros – even if you can't carry a tune – thanks to the *Denonet Singing System*. The Denonet System provides the music and you sing the words. Choose from thousands of tunes to sing along with. You can even record your performance.   *Price: $399*

Pressure Point

Let the *Blood Pressure Monitor* listen to your heart through your finger. Just slip your index finger through the sensor ring, press Start, and moments later, accurate readings of your pulse and blood pressure will appear on the screen.
Price: $169

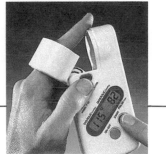

2 Now answer these questions.

a) How is the VOICE Explorer different from other translators?
b) What is an advantage of the minipool?
c) How is the Denonet System different from ordinary recorded music?
d) What does Cafe San have that most coffee makers don't?
e) What two things does the Blood Pressure Monitor measure?

Review of Units 10-12

1 Just what I'm looking for

1 *Pair work* Practice this role play between a rental agent and a client. Cover each other's information.

Student A

You are a rental agent. Someone wants to rent a place to live. You start.

Ask what kind of place the person is looking for and take notes.
You think you have a suitable place. Describe it (make up your own information) and answer any questions.
Then set up a time to show the house or apartment.

Student B

You have moved to a new city and are looking for a place to live. What kind of place do you want? Make notes about: **price range, location, number of bedrooms, facilities, other requirements.**

Now talk to the rental agent. Describe the kind of housing you are looking for.
The agent has something that sounds suitable. Ask for further information about it (for example, kitchen appliances, a parking space, distance from schools, shops).
You'd like to see the place. Set up a time to see it.

2 Now change partners and roles and try the role play again.

2 Chance of a lifetime

1 *Group work* Discuss what you would do in these situations.

a) If you had $50,000 to invest, what would you do?
b) What would you do if you had $100,000 to give away?
c) If you had the chance to start your own business, what kind of business would it be?
d) If you could make a career change, what would it be?
e) If you could trade places with someone for a day, who would it be?
f) Where would you go if you had the chance to live in another country? What would you do there?
g) If you had the chance to change one thing in the world, what would it be?

2 *Class activity* Now compare your suggestions.

3 Listening 📼

Listen to three people complaining about things.
Choose the best response to complete each conversation.

a) .... Oh? What's the matter?
.... Oh. Would you like another one?
.... Oh, I didn't realize that. I'll try to
do something about it.

b) .... Sure. When did you buy it?
.... Oh, yes, they do. You're right.
.... Let me try it on.

c) .... And was the room comfortable?
.... Would you like to pay by check?
.... Sorry. Let me check that for you.

4 Problem solving

1 *Group work* What do you think are the three most serious
problems facing the world today?

A: I think one of the most serious problems is . . . because . . .
B: Getting rid of . . . is another big problem because . . .
C: Well, it seems to me that . . . is a real problem because . . .

2 Now discuss solutions to the problems you identified.

3 *Class activity* Groups compare problems and solutions.

5 Don't throw it away!

1 *Pair work* How many different uses can you think of for these
things?

a bathtub
a wooden door
an old quilt
a car tire
a large mirror

A: What could you do with a bathtub?
B: Well, I think it could be used as a fish pond.
A: And how would you do it?
B: Well, first, you could dig a hole in the yard and
put the bathtub in it. Then . . .

2 *Class activity* Compare your suggestions.

13 That's a possibility

1 SNAPSHOT

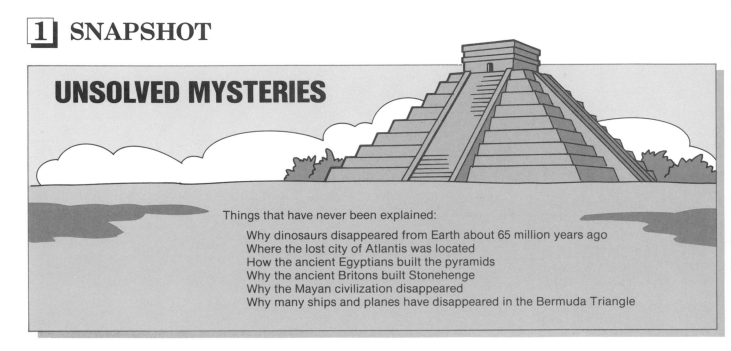

UNSOLVED MYSTERIES

Things that have never been explained:

Why dinosaurs disappeared from Earth about 65 million years ago
Where the lost city of Atlantis was located
How the ancient Egyptians built the pyramids
Why the ancient Britons built Stonehenge
Why the Mayan civilization disappeared
Why many ships and planes have disappeared in the Bermuda Triangle

Discussion
Do you know anything about these mysteries?
Do you know of any other famous unsolved mysteries?
Are there any unsolved mysteries in your country?

2 CONVERSATION 🔊

1 Listen.

A: You know, we're studying dinosaurs in science class. It's really interesting.
B: Oh, yeah? Hey, have you learned why the dinosaurs disappeared?
A: Well, no one knows for sure.
B: I thought it had something to do with the climate. The temperature might have gotten cooler and killed them off.
A: Yeah, that's one theory. Another idea is that they may have run out of food.
B: Uh-huh. And you know, there's even a theory that they could have been destroyed by aliens from outer space.
A: That sounds crazy to me!

2 *Group work* Why do *you* think dinosaurs disappeared?

82

3 PRONUNCIATION: Reduced forms in past modals 📼

1 Listen to how *have* is reduced in these sentences. Then practice them.

The dinosaurs might **have** run out of food.
The wall may **have** prevented floods.

2 Now listen to two more sentences. *Not* is usually not reduced in sentences like these. Practice the sentences.

Atlantis may **not** have been a real city.
The dinosaurs might **not** have been killed by the climate.

4 GRAMMAR FOCUS: Past modals 📼

> They **must have been** killed by the climate.*
> They **could have been** destroyed by aliens.
> They **may have run** out of food.
> There **may not have been** enough water.
> The temperature **might have gotten** cooler.

Note: **Must** shows more certainty than the other modals.

1 Match the information to make sentences. More than one answer for each is possible.

A
a) The ancient Britons may have built Stonehenge
b) The ancient Egyptians could have built the pyramids
c) The dinosaurs might have been killed
d) The Great Wall of China must have been built

B
.... to serve as a place of worship.
.... by hunters.
.... to provide work for people.
.... by visitors from outer space.
.... to serve as landmarks for alien spaceships.
.... by changes in the weather.
.... to keep out invaders.

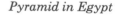

Pyramid in Egypt

2 *Pair work* Read your sentences aloud. Use the reduced form of *have*.

3 Complete the information in column A with your own suggestions. Then compare with a partner.

Stonehenge, England

5 LISTENING 📼

1 Listen to Peter and Marie talking about planes disappearing over the Bermuda Triangle and take notes. What is each person's theory?

2 Now listen to what Sue says about the most recent theory. What does she think might have happened?

3 Why do *you* think the planes disappeared?

6 I'VE OFTEN WONDERED . . .

1 *Group work* Discuss these questions. How many different possibilities can you think of? Then compare suggestions around the class.

How do you think . . .

people paid for things before coins were used as money?
sailors in ancient times knew where they were going?
people had fun before radio and TV were invented?
people communicated before there was the telephone?

Useful expressions

I guess they must have . . .
Do you think they could have . . .?
They probably . . .
They might have . . .

2 *Group work* Now make up a question like the ones above. What suggestions can your classmates give?

7 WORD POWER: Verbs of communication

1 Add these words to the word map.

doubt   guess   laugh   remember   state   tell
forget   joke   mention   remind   tease   think

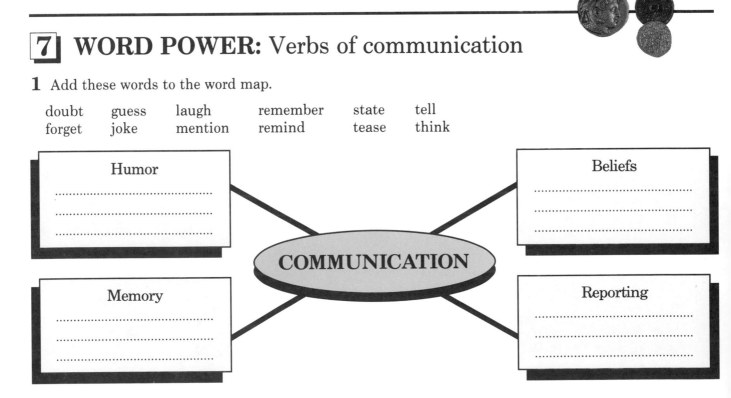

Humor	Beliefs
....	....
....	....
....	....

COMMUNICATION

Memory	Reporting
....	....
....	....
....	....

2 *Pair Work* Can you add two more verbs to each category?

8 CONVERSATION 📼

1 Listen.

A: How was your dinner party?
B: I think it went pretty well.
A: That's good.
B: Yeah, but we shouldn't have invited my wife's boss. We couldn't get him to leave!
A: Really? How late did he stay?
B: Until two o'clock in the morning! And we both had to work the next day.
A: Oh, he shouldn't have stayed so late. That was really inconsiderate. I would have asked him to leave earlier.
B: Well, it's really difficult to say that to your boss!

2 What would you have done in this situation?

9 GRAMMAR FOCUS: Modals and past modals 📼

He **shouldn't have stayed** so late. You **shouldn't have** . . . He **could have been** more considerate. They **might have** . . .	He **should forget** about it. She **shouldn't** . . . They **could** . . . You **might** . . .
I **would have asked** him to leave. I **wouldn't have** . . . I **might have** . . .	I **would apologize**. I **wouldn't** . . . I **might** . . .

Read these situations and make suggestions or comments. Use the expressions above. Then compare with a partner.

a) John's friend borrowed his car and dented it. When he returned it, he didn't say anything to John about it. What would you have done if you were John?

b) Kenji and Kate had planned to get married. At a party, their friends gave them a lot of gifts. Later, Kenji and Kate broke off their engagement; however, they kept the gifts. Do you think they should have kept them?

c) If you received two job offers, one for an interesting job with a low salary and the other for a boring job with a good salary, which job would you take?

10 THAT'S A GOOD QUESTION!

1 *Pair work* Do you sometimes wish you had done things differently in your life? Think of three things and talk about them.

> Well, I probably would have gone to a different university.

> I guess I shouldn't have gotten married so young.

2 Now take turns talking about these situations.

A: What are three things you would never do in public?
B: I'd never wear tennis shoes with a suit, and I'd never . . .

A: What are three things you would refuse to do if someone asked?
B: I'd never tell a lie, and . . .

3 *Class activity* Compare your answers.

11 LISTENING 📼

1 Listen to descriptions of three situations. What would have been the best thing to do in each situation? Check (✓) the best suggestion.

a) .... Dennis should have called a locksmith.
.... He should have called a tow truck.
.... He did the right thing.

b) .... Diana should have turned up her radio to keep out the noise.
.... She should have called the neighbors to see what was happening.
.... She did the right thing.

c) .... Simon should have taken the ring and put an ad in the newspaper.
.... He should have taken the ring and called the police when he got home.
.... He did the right thing.

2 *Pair work* What would you have done?

> ▶ **Interchange 13: Survival**
>
> How well would you survive on the moon? Turn to page 115 and find out.

12 WRITING

1 Write about what you would do in this situation: You have invited a lot of friends to your house for a party, but no one seems to be having fun. Everyone looks bored.

First, I would put on some music and try to get people to dance. Then I would introduce people to each other . . .

2 *Pair work* Now exchange papers and compare your suggestions.

13 READING: The case of the missing pilot

On October 21, 1978, Australian pilot Frederick Valentich, age 20, took off from Melbourne and headed toward a small island. It was the young man's first solo night flight over water. It was a still, clear evening, and from his Cessna aircraft Valentich had a perfect view of the sky above and the sea below.

Shortly after taking off, however, Valentich reported to flight controllers in Melbourne that he was being followed by a UFO. "It's a long shape," he reported, "with a green light, sort of metallic-like, all shiny on the outside." A few minutes later, he told the controllers, "That strange aircraft is hovering on top of me again." After that, Valentich stopped talking. For the next fourteen seconds the traffic controllers heard a strange ringing sound. Then silence. Valentich and his plane never reached the island, and no trace of him or his aircraft was ever found.

Several members of the public reported seeing strange phenomena in the sky over Melbourne that night. An amateur photographer produced a photo of what looked like a large object surrounded by vapor. A NASA scientist, Richard Haines, heard about the story and began an investigation. He analyzed Valentich's voice on tape and the strange sound heard at the end of the tape. But he concluded that it was "unidentifiable." He decided that there were four possible explanations for the mystery surrounding Valentich's disappearance: (1) Valentich might have become confused and disoriented while flying his plane and finally crashed; (2) he could have staged a deliberate hoax; (3) he could have been the victim of a top secret advanced weapons test; or (4) he may have been captured by the occupants of a UFO.

Haines plans to continue with his investigation of the case until the mystery is solved.

a) Was Valentich an experienced pilot?
b) What do you think the ringing sound that the controllers heard might have been?
c) Which of Haines's theories do you think is the most likely explanation?
d) Can you think of another explanation for what might have happened?

14 The right stuff

1 SNAPSHOT

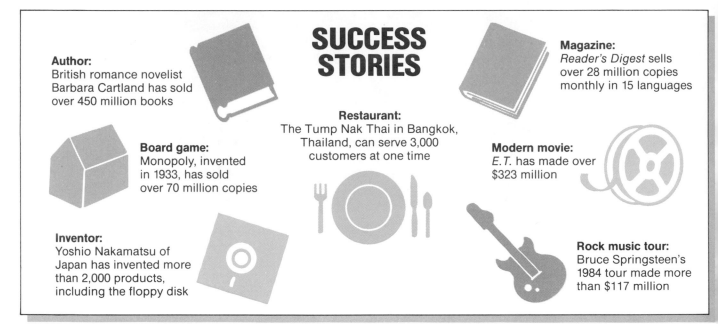

SUCCESS STORIES

Author:
British romance novelist Barbara Cartland has sold over 450 million books

Board game:
Monopoly, invented in 1933, has sold over 70 million copies

Inventor:
Yoshio Nakamatsu of Japan has invented more than 2,000 products, including the floppy disk

Restaurant:
The Tump Nak Thai in Bangkok, Thailand, can serve 3,000 customers at one time

Magazine:
Reader's Digest sells over 28 million copies monthly in 15 languages

Modern movie:
E.T. has made over $323 million

Rock music tour:
Bruce Springsteen's 1984 tour made more than $117 million

Discussion
What is your favorite movie, magazine, and novel?
Name three successful people. Why do you think they are successful?

2 WORD POWER: Adjectives

1 *Pair work*   What qualities are important for the following?
Add two more adjectives to each list, and then rank them from 1 to 7.

A successful magazine	*A successful inventor*	*A successful businessperson*
.... cheap	.... creative	.... clever
.... entertaining	.... independent	.... dynamic
.... informative	.... intelligent	.... friendly
.... useful	.... patient	.... hardworking
.... well written	.... practical	.... tough
....	....	....
....	....	....

2 List three qualities that are most important for each of these things
to be successful. Compare answers around the class.

   a TV program   an advertisement   a salesperson

3 GRAMMAR FOCUS: Sentences with *if*-clauses and infinitives 🔲

> | | |
> |---|---|
> | **If you want to be a writer,** | you need to have a good imagination. |
> | **To be successful in business,** | you have to be tough. |
> | **In order to be an inventor,** | you must be creative. |
> | **For a movie to be successful,** | it should have a good story. |

1 Match the information to make sentences.

A

a) If you want to have a successful restaurant,
b) In order to be an effective teacher,
c) For a TV commercial to be effective,
d) If you want to throw a successful party,
e) To make a good impression during a job interview,
f) In order to be a good parent,

B

.... it has to have good camera work.
.... you must have an excellent chef.
.... you should spend a lot of time with your children.
.... you ought to provide good music and snacks.
.... it's important to know your subject thoroughly.
.... you need to dress well and be punctual.

2 Now complete column A with information of your own. Then compare with a partner.

Drawing by C. Barsotti; © 1989 The New Yorker Magazine, Inc.

4 PRONUNCIATION: Reduced forms 🔲

1 Notice how the following words are reduced in conversation. Listen and repeat.

"a" = /ə/	**a** successful restaurant
"an" = /ən/	**an** effective teacher
"and" = /ənd/ *or* /ən/	interesting **and** useful
	cheap **and** entertaining
"of" = /əv/	a lot **of** time
"to" = /tə/	ought **to** go
	have **to** come

2 Now listen and practice the sentences in Exercise 3.1, and pay attention to reduced forms.

5 LISTENING 📼

1 Listen to a student talking to a career counselor about a job interview and take notes. What are the things the counselor considers important about a job interview?

2 *Pair work* Compare your notes. Do you agree with the counselor's suggestions? Do you have any other suggestions?

6 WHAT DOES IT TAKE?

1 *Group work* Talk about some of the things below or topics of your own. What are the most important things you need:

a) to run a successful language school, hotel, or business?

b) to be a successful actor or actress, doctor, or musician?

2 *Class activity* Now compare your answers.

7 WRITING

Eaton Centre in Toronto, Canada

1 Choose one of the topics in Exercise 6 or a similar topic. First make notes and then write a composition.

> To develop a successful shopping center, there are four important things to consider: the location, the shops and stores, other facilities, and parking.
>
> The location is very important. The shopping center should ...
>
> The kinds of stores in the shopping center are also important. There should be ...
>
> The shopping center should also include other facilities, such as ...
>
> Parking is another important consideration. Shoppers need ...
>
> These are some of the things you need to consider if you want to have a successful shopping center.

2 *Group work* Now read each other's compositions. Can you give any suggestions?

8 CONVERSATION 📼

1 Listen.

A: Look at this interesting ad! What do you think it's advertising?
B: Gee, it looks like an ad for a car.
A: Mmm, try again.
B: Well, it could be an ad for clothes. But whatever it's selling, it's a great photograph.
A: Yeah. It really caught my eye!

2 What do you think the ad is for? Role-play the conversation using your own information. (The answer is on page 134.)

9 CATCHY SLOGANS

1 *Pair work* Look at these slogans from advertisements. What products do you think they are advertising?

Designed to be seen and not heard.
Quality is Job 1.
Don't leave home without it.
We cover the four corners of the Earth.
Because your signature deserves the best.

Useful expressions
I think it might be
   advertising . . .
This could be an ad for . . .
That's used in the . . . ads.

2 *Class activity* Compare your suggestions. (Answers are on page 132.)

10 A PICTURE IS WORTH A THOUSAND WORDS

1 *Group work* Look at these ads. What do you think each one is
advertising? (Answers are on page 133.)

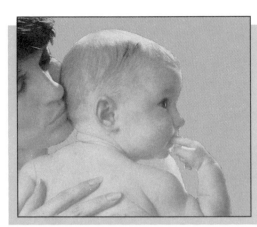

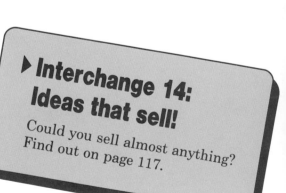

2 Do you think the ads are effective? Why or why not?
Talk about these things.

the concept or idea used in the ad   the layout or design
the photography   the slogan or words used
the use of color

3 *Class activity* Now compare answers.

11 LISTENING 📼

1 Listen to this radio commercial. What do you
think is being advertised?

2 Listen again and answer these questions.

Where is the conversation taking place?
What does the woman say about her son?
What does the commercial tell you about the
   product?
Do you think the humor in this commercial is
   effective? Why or why not?

▶ Interchange 14:
Ideas that sell!
Could you sell almost anything?
Find out on page 117.

12 READING: New ideas in advertising

In Japan, several different ways of advertising products are used. Here are a few examples.

Effective TV Commercials

One advertising technique used on Japanese television is to play the exact same commercial twice in a row without a pause. Such commercials are usually short, loud, and cheaply made. The less professional-looking the commercial, the more effective it becomes when shown twice.

Giveaways

What better way to get people to pay attention to you than to give them something that has your message on it, that is free and practical, and that they'll carry around with them and use often? The most common giveaway in Japan is packets of tissue paper. Why? Perhaps because many public restrooms in Japan don't provide paper towels.

Video Billboards on Wheels

Used frequently by Japanese liquor and cosmetics companies, Mobotron is a giant VCR on wheels with a screen measuring 10 by 13 feet (3 by 4 meters). It is rented by the day and can go anywhere. It can be driven through city streets with the video and soundtrack playing, or it can be stationed at locations such as a golf course, school, company sports event, or convention.

a) Do you think each of the techniques above is effective? Why or why not?

b) Can you think of any disadvantages to these types of advertising?

c) Can you think of three interesting advertising techniques used in your country?

15 It's a matter of opinion

1 SNAPSHOT

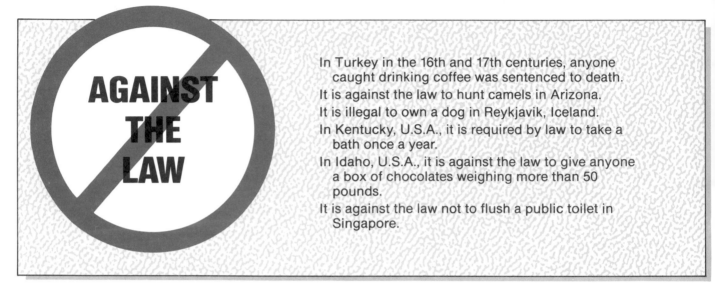

In Turkey in the 16th and 17th centuries, anyone caught drinking coffee was sentenced to death.

It is against the law to hunt camels in Arizona.

It is illegal to own a dog in Reykjavik, Iceland.

In Kentucky, U.S.A., it is required by law to take a bath once a year.

In Idaho, U.S.A., it is against the law to give anyone a box of chocolates weighing more than 50 pounds.

It is against the law not to flush a public toilet in Singapore.

Discussion
Can you think of reasons for any one of these laws?
Do you know of any other strange laws?

2 CONVERSATION 🔲

1 Listen.

A: How was your vacation?
B: It was OK, but every time I lit up a cigarette, someone asked me to stop smoking. I'm getting sick of all these restrictions! I think we should be able to smoke wherever we like in public.
A: Well, I don't know. Non-smokers have their rights, too, you know. I hate breathing other people's smoke.
B: Mmm. Maybe someday there'll be a smokeless cigarette, and then everyone will be happy.

THANK YOU FOR NOT SMOKING

2 *Role play* Close your books and have a conversation like the one above. One person is *for* smoking in public and the other *against* it.

3 *Discussion* Do you think smoking should be banned in all public places (for example, offices, restaurants, airplanes), or do you think smokers should be free to smoke wherever they want?

94

3 LISTENING 📼

1 Listen to Steve telling Carmen his opinions about portable stereos and bicycles. What does he say about each one?

2 Listen again. What does Carmen think?

4 GIVING OPINIONS

1 Notice how we can give opinions and respond to them.

Giving an opinion

I think . . .
I really think . . .
I don't think . . .

Acknowledging an opinion

Really?
Oh, do you think so?
Well, it's a matter of opinion.

Asking for reasons

Do you? Why? *or* Don't you? Why not?
Why do you say that?
Really? Why not?

Giving reasons

Well, because . . . And another thing, . . .
Yes, because I think that . . .

2 *Pair work* Take turns discussing the statements below.
Have conversations like this.

A: I think all courses in school should be
   graded Pass/Fail.
B: Really? Why?
A: Well, because . . .

A: I don't think all courses should be graded
   Pass/Fail.
B: Don't you? Why not?
A: Well, for one thing, . . .

#1 All courses in school should be graded Pass/Fail.
#2 There should be no restrictions on travel anywhere in the world.
#3 Companies should provide free day care for employees' children.
#4 When buses or trains are delayed, passengers should get a free ride.
#5 Everyone should have free health care.

3 *Group work* Write three statements like the ones above.
Then discuss them with your classmates.

5 GRAMMAR FOCUS: Tag questions and responses 🔘

Parking **is** difficult here, **isn't** it?	Yes, it **is**.
Houses **aren't** cheap these days, **are** they?	No, they **aren't**.
Taxis here **are** expensive, **aren't** they?	Yes, they **are**.
This town **has** terrible traffic, **doesn't** it?	Yes, it **does**.
They **don't** drive very well here, **do** they?	No, they **don't**.
Stores downtown **charge** high prices, **don't** they?	Yes, they **do**.
You **can't** find cheap housing here, **can** you?	No, you **can't**.
They **should** make gambling illegal, **shouldn't** they?	Yes, they **should**.

This town has terrible traffic, doesn't it?

Add tag questions to these statements.

a) Prices these days keep going up, . . .?
b) Drivers here aren't very courteous, . . .?
c) The subways are getting really crowded, . . .?
d) Traffic downtown is getting worse, . . .?
e) It isn't easy to save money anymore, . . .?
f) Sales taxes should be abolished, . . .?

---

6 PRONUNCIATION: Intonation in tag questions 🔘

1 We use falling intonation in tag questions when we expect someone to agree with us.

Parking is difficult here, isn't it?

2 Now listen and practice the sentences you added tags to in Exercise 5.

---

7 IT REALLY BUGS ME!

1 What are some things people feel strongly about in your school or city? Write four statements using tag questions.

2 *Group work* Now take turns reading your statements. Use falling intonation in the tag questions. Others make responses.

A: The food in the cafeteria is terrible, isn't it?
B: Yes, it is. They should get a new cook!

8 WORD POWER: Definitions

1 Match each word with a definition. Then compare with a partner.

a) criticize	.... say you will not do something that you are
b) deny	asked to do
c) propose	.... tell someone what they should do about
d) advise	something
e) congratulate	.... point out the faults of someone or
f) refuse	something
g) apologize	.... say you are sorry for doing something wrong
h) contradict	.... suggest an idea for people to think about
	.... give an opposite opinion about something or
	someone
	.... praise people for their success or for a happy
	event
	.... say that something is not true

2 *Pair work* Now choose four of the words above and use them in sentences.

You always criticize my cooking. Next time, cook your
own dinner!

9 LISTENING 🔊

1 Listen to people giving their opinions about current issues in the news. What issues are they talking about?

a) ....

....

b) ....

....

2 Now listen again and take notes. What opinions do you hear for and against each issue? Compare with a partner.

3 *Group work* What do you think about these issues?

10 EXPRESSING DISAGREEMENT

1 Notice how we can disagree with opinions.

Acknowledging an opinion and offering a different one

Yeah, that's interesting, but I think . . .
That may be true. However, . . .
That's a good point, but . . .
Well, maybe, but don't you think that . . .?

Disagreeing with an opinion and offering a different one

Oh, I don't know. I feel that . . .
I disagree. I think . . .
Well, I don't think that's true . . .
I don't see it that way at all. I think that . . .

Ending a discussion

Mmm. I guess we just have different opinions.
Well, maybe. I'll have to think about it.
I guess we can't agree on this.

2 *Group work* Take turns discussing these statements. Use some of the expressions above.

a) Fifty percent of all government officials should be women.
b) All nuclear power plants should be banned.
c) School should be voluntary after the age of twelve years.
d) All public transportation should be free.

11 ARE YOU KIDDING?

1 Write a statement giving your opinion on a current issue.

2 *Group work* Now take turns reading your statements and giving your reasons. Others agree or disagree.

Useful expressions

Are you kidding?
Come on!
Do you really believe that?

12 WRITING

1 Write a composition about one of the topics you discussed in this unit. Give your opinion about the topic and your reasons. Don't put your name on your composition.

2 *Class activity* Put your compositions on the bulletin board. Can you guess who wrote each one?

13 READING: Animal rights

Can you think of three reasons for and three reasons against using animals in medical research?

Now read the passage and then answer the questions below.

Every year about seventeen million animals are used in laboratory experiments. But in many countries today, a difficult question is being asked: Do we have the right to use animals this way?

The case for using animals in research

The use of animals in medical research has many practical benefits. Animal research has enabled researchers to develop treatments for many diseases, such as heart disease and depression. It would not have been possible to develop vaccines for diseases like smallpox and polio without animal research. Every drug anyone takes today was tried first on animals.

Future medical research is dependent on the use of animals. Which is more important: the life of a rat or that of a three-year-old child?

Medical research is also an excellent way of using unwanted animals. Last year, over twelve million animals had to be killed in animal shelters because nobody wanted them as pets.

The case against using animals in research

The fact that humans benefit cannot be used to justify using animals in research any more than it can be used to justify experimenting on other humans. Animals suffer a lot during these experiments. They are forced to live in small cages, and they may be unable to move.

Much of the research that is carried out is unnecessary anyway.

Animals have the same rights as humans do – to be able to move freely and not to have pain or fear forced on them. Researchers must find other ways of doing their research, using cell culture and computer modeling. There should be no animals in research laboratories at all.

a) Which of the arguments is more convincing – the case for or the case against the use of animals in medical research?
b) What is your opinion on using animals for research?

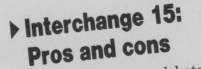

▶ **Interchange 15: Pros and cons**

Are you ready for a debate? Turn to page 118 and find out.

Review of Units 13–15

1 Inheritance

Pair work   You have just inherited $500,000. Take turns talking about what you would do with the money. Ask these questions and others of your own.

Would you quit school or your job?
What would you buy?
Would you give any of the money away?
Would you take a trip anywhere? Would you take anyone with you?
What changes to your life-style do you think you might make?
Would you invest some of the money? How?
What else would you do?

2 Listening ▭

Listen to four people talking about things that happened to them.

Where do the conversations take place?
What do you think might have happened?

Talk about them like this.

They might have . . .   She must have . . .
He could have . . .   I think they probably . . .

3 The perfect match

1 *Group work*   What are the five most important ingredients for a successful marriage? Talk about them like this.

A: For a marriage to be successful, the husband/wife must . . .
B: The husband/wife should always . . .
C: If you want to be a good husband/wife, . . .

2 *Class activity*   Compare your suggestions.

4 New slogan

1 *Pair work*   You have been hired by an ad agency. Can you think of an interesting slogan for each of these products?

2 *Class activity*   Compare your slogans. Who has the best slogan for each product?

5 Listening 📼

Listen to people giving opinions, and choose the correct response.

a) .... Yes, it is.
    .... Yes, it was.
    .... Yes, you can.

b) .... Yes, they do.
    .... Yes, it does.
    .... Yes, they should.

c) .... Yes, it is.
    .... Yes, we do.
    .... Yes, it does.

d) .... Yes, it does.
    .... Yes, they are.
    .... Yes, you can.

e) .... No, you can't.
    .... No, they aren't.
    .... No, they don't.

f) .... No, they don't.
    .... No, it isn't.
    .... No, you can't.

6 There ought to be a law

1 *Pair work*   Think of a law you would like to see passed in your city.

> They should pass a law that . . .
> There should be a law against . . .
> I think . . . should be banned.

2 *Group work*   Tell the group your suggestion and discuss it.
Do the other students agree or disagree?

Interchange Activities

Hidden truths

Class activity Go around the class and use the cues below to ask questions:

Do you speak three languages?

When someone answers "Yes," write down his or her name. Then ask a follow-up question and make notes:

What languages do you speak?

Continue until you have a name for each question.

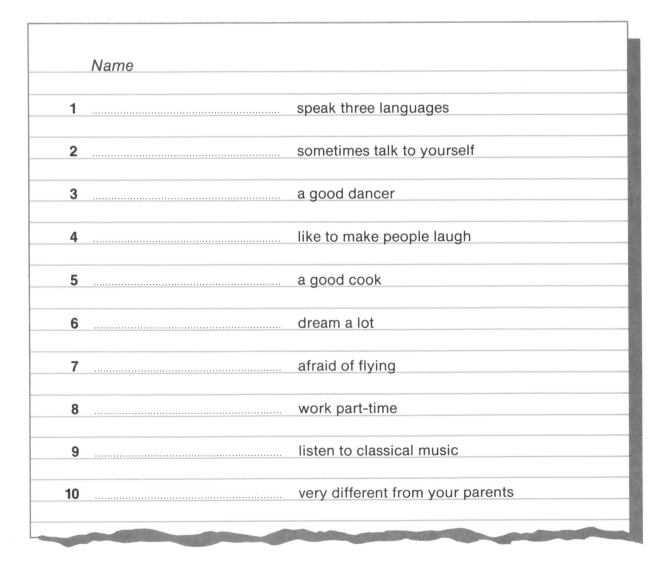

	Name	
1	....	speak three languages
2	....	sometimes talk to yourself
3	....	a good dancer
4	....	like to make people laugh
5	....	a good cook
6	....	dream a lot
7	....	afraid of flying
8	....	work part-time
9	....	listen to classical music
10	....	very different from your parents

Now take turns. Report the most interesting answers to the class.

Interchange 2 | I'd like that job!

Preparation

1 *Group work* Work in groups of four. You are members of a company or organization. You need to hire some new employees. First, decide on the type of company you work for. Then write four different job ads on separate cards for interesting positions in your company.

PORTERVILLE DAILY MAIL
is looking for a

FILM CRITIC

Must have a background in journalism and good knowledge of the movie industry. Contact Bruce for an interview.

2 *Class activity* Now half of the groups put their job ads on the bulletin board. The rest of the students each choose a job ad and take it to the company to have an interview.

The Job Interview

3 Now the group interviews the job applicants one at a time. Ask questions like these and others of your own.

> Why did you apply for this job?
>
> Tell us about your educational background.
>
> Why do you think you'd be good for this job?
> Do you have any experience in this kind of work?
> Do you have any special skills? What are they?
> How well can you . . .?
> Are you good at . . .?
>
> What do you think are your strengths and personal qualities?
>
> Why are you leaving your present job?
>
> Do you have any questions you'd like to ask us?

Finish the interview like this:

> Thank you very much for coming today.
> We'll be in touch.

4 Now the other groups put their job ads on the bulletin board, and the class tries the activity again.

Interchange 3 The best and the worst

1 *Group work* Choose a city or town you all know well. What are the six things you like most about it? Talk about them like this.

> One good thing is the weather.
> It's great in the summer.
> The best thing for me is the food.
> There're lots of good restaurants.
> It doesn't have much pollution.

Now rank the six best things from 1 to 6, and write them below.

The best things in .... *(city or town)*

1 ....

2 ....

3 ....

4 ....

5 ....

6 ....

2 Talk about the things you don't like about the city or town.

> The thing I hate most is the weather
>   in the winter.
> The worst thing is the crowded subways.
> There are not enough parks.
> There's no place for kids to play.

Now rank the six worst things from 1 to 6, and write them below.

The worst things in .... *(city or town)*

1 ....

2 ....

3 ....

4 ....

5 ....

6 ....

3 *Class activity* Tell the class about the best and the worst things in the city you talked about.

Interchange 4 | A double ending – STUDENTS A and B

1 *Pair work* Read the beginning and end of this story. What do you think happened during the middle part of it? Tell the rest of the story. Make notes.

Ken Passell was born in Columbus, Ohio. He came from a large, working-class family. His father worked in a flour mill, and his mother was a factory worker. When Ken was a child, he was very good with his hands.

....

....

....

....

....

....

....

....

....

The wedding was held in the biggest church in Los Angeles. Then Ken and Cindy left on their private yacht for a honeymoon cruise to Baja, Mexico. When they return, they will live in their 20-room mansion in Beverly Hills.

2 *Group work* Now tell your story to Students C and D and answer any questions they have. Then listen to their story.

Interchange 4 | A double ending – STUDENTS C and D

1 *Pair work*   Read the beginning and end of this story. What do you
think happened during the middle part of it? Tell the rest of the story.
Make notes.

Ken Passell was born in Columbus, Ohio. He came
from a large, working-class family. His father
worked in a flour mill, and his mother was a
factory worker. When Ken was a child, he was very
good with his hands.

....
....
....
....
....
....
....
....
....
....

Ken and his wife Cindy were arrested last week in
London. They had over $250,000 in cash in a
suitcase, and Cindy was wearing over $100,000 in
jewelry. Inspector Quinn said, "This is one of the
most bizarre cases I have ever been involved with."

2 *Group work*   Now listen to Students A and B tell their story. Ask
any questions you want. Then tell them your story.

Interchange 5 | **You must be kidding!**

1 Think of an unusual request (the kind of request you hope you never get!) and write it like this:

> Would you mind if some relatives of mine stayed with you for a few days? My uncle and aunt and their four young children are coming to town this week, and I really don't have room for them.

2 *Class activity* Go around the class and make your request to three different classmates. Each person you ask declines the request and gives an unusual excuse.

> Oh, I'd really love to, but the Smithville Ladies' Baseball League is visiting town next week, and six of them are staying in my apartment. Maybe some other time.

Write down the reason each person gives.

Carmen's excuse:

> The Smithville Ladies' Baseball League is visiting town next week. Six of them are staying in her apartment.

3 Who gave the best excuse? Report it to the class like this:

This was my request:

> "Would you mind if some relatives of mine . . . ?"

Carmen gave the best excuse:

> "The Smithville Ladies' Baseball League is visiting town . . ."

Interchange 6 | Shopping survey

1 Read each question in the survey and circle your preference. Then write a short reason for your choice.

Shopping Survey

Reason

a) When shopping, would you rather
   (1) use a credit card   *or*
   (2) pay with cash?

b) If you wanted to replace all your furniture
   in your home, would you prefer
   (1) getting a loan   *or*
   (2) saving up the necessary money for it?

c) Do you prefer shopping
   (1) in a large department store   *or*
   (2) in a small specialty store?

d) When you are buying clothes, which is more important:
   (1) choosing a famous designer label   *or*
   (2) considering the price tag?

e) If you wanted to move, would you rather
   (1) sell the things you don't want anymore   *or*
   (2) just throw them away?

f) Which do you prefer:
   (1) borrowing money from a bank   *or*
   (2) asking a friend you know for a loan?

g) If you wanted to buy a home, would you rather
   (1) buy an old house and fix it up   *or*
   (2) buy a modern new house?

h) Which kind of car would you rather buy:
   (1) a domestic car   *or*
   (2) a foreign car?

i) When you want to thank someone for something, do you prefer
   (1) buying the person a gift   *or*
   (2) taking the person out to dinner?

2 Now interview two classmates and write down their preferences and reasons.

3 *Class activity*   Compare your answers.

Interchange 7 | Studying abroad

1 Every year, many students go abroad to study. These are some of the things they have to think about. Look at the questions below and then add three more to each list.

Part 1: Getting ready

a) What subjects are good ones to study abroad?
b) Which countries are good places to study these subjects?
c) How can you get more information about studying abroad?
d) Where can you get information about scholarships?
e) How do you enroll in a foreign school?
f) What are the main things you have to do before you leave?
g) What things will you need to take with you?

Your questions:

1 ....
2 ....
3 ....

Part 2: After you're there

a) Where can you stay when you first arrive?
b) What kinds of things will you have to buy?
c) How can you get information about housing in the city?
d) Is it better to stay in a dormitory or with a family? Why?
e) Where could you get extra help in studying the language?

Your questions:

1 ....
2 ....
3 ....

2 *Group work* Now discuss the questions. One person is the group secretary and takes notes.

3 *Class activity* Compare your answers.

Interchange 8 | Do you have a minute?

1 *Class activity* Where can you do these things (a–l) in your city or town? Talk to three people and get as much information as you can. Take notes.

Where's a good place to . . .?

a) try good local food
b) see people making handicrafts
c) go shopping
d) learn about the history of the area
e) see local theater
f) hear musicians play
g) see interesting architecture
h) take vistors from out-of-town
i) go out on a date
j) play sports
k) go on a day trip
l) go hiking

2 How many of the things that people suggested have you done?

Interchange 9 | History buff – STUDENT A

1 Take turns asking these questions. Check (✓) if your partner gives the correct answer. (The correct answers are underlined.)

1 Was Julius Caesar emperor of Athens, <u>Rome</u>, or Constantinople?
2 What nationality was Alexander the Great? Was he Egyptian, Roman, or <u>Greek</u>?
3 Where did the Mayas live? Was it in Central Europe, <u>North and Central America</u>, or Southeast Asia?
4 In which year did Mexico gain its independence? Was it in 1721, <u>1821</u>, or 1921?
5 When did World War I take place? Was it from 1898 to 1903, or from 1911 to 1915, or <u>from 1914 to 1918</u>?
6 Which was the first country to abolish slavery? Was it Britain, <u>Denmark</u>, or Spain?
7 What city was the first permanent settlement in Canada? Was it Toronto, Montreal, or <u>Quebec</u>?
8 Who wrote the novel <u>1984</u>? Was it <u>George Orwell</u>, H.G. Wells, or Oscar Wilde?
9 When were the first CDs put on the market? Was it in 1963, 1973, <u>1983</u>?
10 Was Cleopatra the Queen of Rome, <u>Egypt</u>, or Greece?

Who has the most correct answers?

2 *Pair work* Now think of five more questions of your own. Can the rest of the class answer them?

Interchange 10 | You sold me a piece of junk! – STUDENT A

Role play

1 You bought some things from an appliance and electronics store that sells used goods. When you took them home, you found there were problems with them. Take them back to the store and explain the problems. Try to get your money back. Use the information below and other information of your own.

a) You bought a cassette player. It doesn't work right. It damages the cassette tapes.
b) You also bought a portable color television. The color control doesn't work. The picture is only in black and white.

2 Now change partners and roles. This time you are the salesperson in the store. A customer comes into the store and complains about the things he or she bought. You are sure the things were working right when you sold them. Because you sell used items, they don't come with a guarantee. Listen to the customer's complaints and decide what you will do, if anything.

Interchange 9 | History buff – STUDENT B

1 Take turns asking these questions. Check (✓) if your partner gives the correct answer. (The correct answers are underlined.)

1 Who was the president of the United States after Lyndon Johnson? Was it Jimmy Carter, <u>Richard Nixon</u>, or Ronald Reagan?
2 Which country did the <u>Han Dynasty</u> rule? Was it <u>China</u>, India, or Japan?
3 Was Britain's Queen Victoria the mother, grandmother, or <u>great-great-grandmother</u> of Queen Elizabeth?
4 Who was the first American woman in space? Was it Stella Quinn, <u>Sally Ride</u>, or Sylvia Warren?
5 When did Walt Disney make his first cartoon movie? Was it in 1920, <u>1938</u>, or 1947?
6 In which century did the composer Mozart live? Was it the 17th, <u>18th</u>, or 19th century?
7 Who was the novel *Frankenstein* written by? Was it Jane Austen, John Keats, or <u>Mary Shelley</u>?
8 What was the actress Marilyn Monroe's real name? Was it <u>Norma Jean Baker</u>, Mary Lou Dreyer, or Billy Jean Monkton?
9 When was the first Volkswagen car built? Was it in the 1920s, <u>the 1930s</u>, or the 1940s?
10 Who used the first magnetic compass? Was it the Americans, <u>the Chinese</u>, or the Dutch?

Who has the most correct answers?

2 *Pair work* Now think of five more questions of your own. Can the rest of the class answer them?

Interchange 10 | You sold me a piece of junk! – STUDENT B

Role play

1 You work in an appliance and electronics store that sells used things. Everything in the store is really cheap, but there are no guarantees on the condition of the appliances you sell. A customer comes into the store and complains about the goods he or she bought. You are sure the things were working right when you sold them. Listen to the customer's complaints and decide what you will do, if anything.

2 Now change partners and roles. It's your turn to be the customer. You bought some things from the appliance and electronics store. When you took them home, you found there were problems with them. Take them back to the store and explain the problems. Try to get your money back. Use the information below and other information of your own.

a) You bought a hair dryer. The handle gets too hot when you use it.
b) You also bought a camera. The lens has a scratch on it.

Interchange 11 And how about you?

Group work Take turns saying what you would do in each of these situations. Then choose the best solution for each one.

Useful expressions

I think I would . . .
I guess I'd . . .
The best thing to do would be to . . .
I might . . .
I really don't know what I would do.

a) You're having a picnic in a public park. You notice another group of people about to leave, but they are leaving all their trash on the ground.

b) You're driving along a busy freeway. You notice that the back wheel of the car in front of you is nearly flat.

c) You've been invited to your boss's house for dinner. An elaborate meal has been prepared, but you find you don't like anything that is being served.

d) You leave a sports bag in a locker room. You go back a couple of days later, but it's not there. A few weeks later, you notice someone else using your bag.

e) You take a camera to a store to be repaired. When you pick it up, the store gives you a different – and better – camera by mistake.

f) A co-worker in your office keeps trying to invite you out. You don't really like this person.

g) Someone gives you an expensive gift, but you don't like it and have no use for it.

h) You live in an apartment building. At 3 A.M., you hear a scream and strange banging noises followed by breaking glass in the apartment below.

Interchange 12 | Same or different? – STUDENT A

Take turns describing and identifying things. One student describes an item, and the other tries to identify which of four things is being described.

1 You start. Describe this item. Give as much information as you can about it and answer your partner's questions.

2 Now listen to your partner's description of an item. Ask questions to try to identify which of the following items it is.

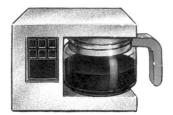   

3 Describe this item.

4 Now identify which item your partner is describing.

Interchange 13 | Survival

1 *Group work* You are a group of astronauts on the moon.
Unfortunately, you have become separated from your base camp. You
have the following things with you. First, discuss how important each
thing is for your survival, and then what each thing could be used for.

.... box of matches
.... food concentrate
.... 50 feet of nylon rope
.... parachute silk
.... portable heating unit
.... two pistols
.... one case of dehydrated milk
.... two 100-pound tanks of oxygen
.... map of the stars as seen from the moon
.... life raft
.... magnetic compass
.... five gallons of water
.... signal flares
.... first-aid kit
.... solar-powered receiver-transmitter

Well, we could use the box of matches to . . .
I don't think we would need the . . .
The . . . would be very important because
 we could use it to . . .

Now rank the items above from 1 to 15 in the order of their importance
for your survival.

2 *Class activity* Compare your lists and discuss the differences.

[This survival game was first developed by the National Aeronautics and
Space Administration (NASA). When you complete the activity, look at
page 134 and compare your list with theirs.]

Interchange 12 | Same or different? – STUDENT B

Take turns describing and identifying things. One student describes an
item, and the other tries to identify which of four things is being described.

1 Listen to your partner's description of an item. Ask questions to try
to identify which of the following items it is.

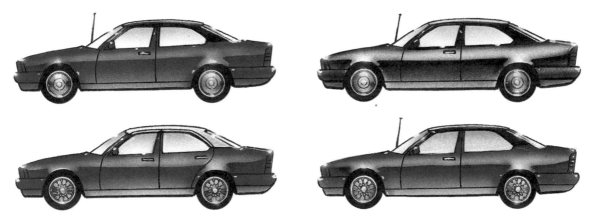

2 Now it's your turn. Describe this item. Give as much information as
you can about it and answer your partner's questions.

3 Identify which item your partner is describing.

4 Now describe this item.

Interchange 14 Ideas that sell!

1 *Group work* You work for an advertising agency. Write a 30-second radio or TV commercial for one of the following products. Use some of the information below and other information of your own.

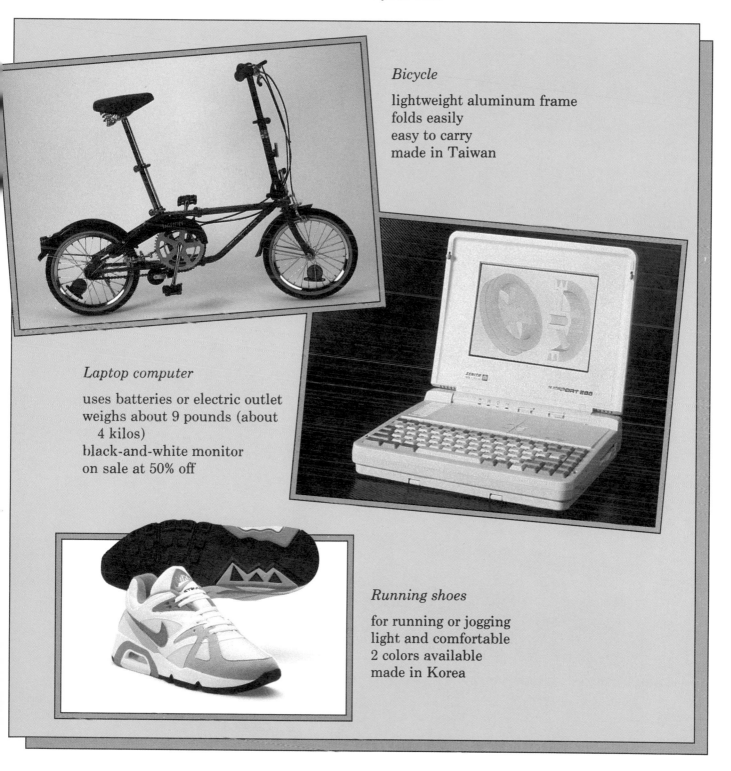

Bicycle

lightweight aluminum frame
folds easily
easy to carry
made in Taiwan

Laptop computer

uses batteries or electric outlet
weighs about 9 pounds (about
   4 kilos)
black-and-white monitor
on sale at 50% off

Running shoes

for running or jogging
light and comfortable
2 colors available
made in Korea

2 *Class activity* Each group reads its commercial to the class. Which group has the best commercial?

Interchange 15 | Pros and cons

Preparation

You are going to have a debate. Two teams will choose a controversial topic and then discuss it from opposite points of view.

1 *Group work* Form two teams of 4 or 5 students each. Each team chooses a team captain. Use a topic below or another of your own.

Every citizen should serve in the army for 3 years after graduating from school.

Office workers should be allowed to listen to music on personal stereos while they work.

Rock albums that contain lyrics about violence should be packaged with a warning label.

Tourism brings more harm than good to developing countries.

Then decide which position your team will take – to be either *for* or *against* the topic.

2 Now the two teams work separately to prepare for the debate. One team prepares its arguments *for* the proposition, and the other team prepares its arguments *against* it. During the debate, each student on the team has to present one of the team's arguments and give reasons that support the team's position.

The debate

3 *Class activity* Take turns having debates. After both teams present their arguments, the rest of the class decides which team has won (that is, has the best arguments).

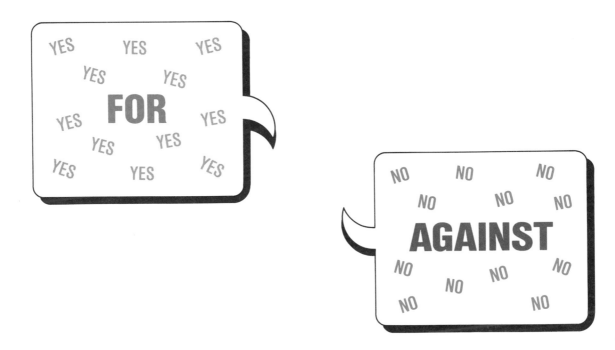

Unit Summaries

Unit 1 That's what friends are for

Grammar

1. Position of clauses with WHO and THAT

> **In subject position**
> **People who talk loudly** bother me.
> **Dogs that bark during the night** drive me crazy.
>
> **In object position**
> I don't like **people who talk loudly.**
> I can't stand **dogs that bark loudly.**

2. Position of clauses with WHEN

> **In initial position**
> **When people arrive late for appointments,** I get very angry.
>
> **In final position**
> I get very angry **when people arrive late for appointments.**

Key Vocabulary

Nouns
ad (advertisement)
advice
appointment
best friend
boyfriend
briefcase
cherry pie
challenge
classical music
college
contents
cook
couple
course
dancer
fast food
feelings
flying
girlfriend
gum
help
high school
hurry
importance
junior high school
language
opinion
parents
partner
personality
primary school
relationship
restaurant

roommate
smoke
sport
subject
terms
terms of endearment

Verbs
bake
blow
bother
call
chew
cut class
dream
enjoy
expect
fail
finish
get along with
get back
get upset
hate
interrupt
laugh
leave
listen
look for
lose
love
show
speak
steal

talk
teach
travel
wait
watch
work
worry

Adjectives
ambitious
best
both
depressed
different
disgusting
easygoing
emotional
favorite
funny
generous
gloomy
honest
impatient
important
independent
interested
late
moody
most
other
part-time
patient
perfect

punctual
proud
reliable
selfish
similar
sociable
unreliable
wrong

Adverbs
all over the place
always
at once
calmly
easily
fairly
often
really
so
sometimes

Conjunction
while

Expressions
I can't stand it!
Guess what?

Unit 2 On the job

Grammar

Gerunds and **-ing** clauses

As subject
Teaching is an interesting career.
Teaching children is an interesting career.

As direct object
I enjoy **teaching**.
I enjoy **working with children**.

As subject complement
My first job was **teaching in a primary school**.
My first job was **selling computers.**

Key Vocabulary

Nouns
accountant
adding machine
airline pilot
air travel
benefits
bonus
clerk
commission
computer
construction worker
construction site
deadline
earnings
educational background
engineer
experience
evening
family member
flight attendant
health insurance
homemaker
homework
information
interview
journalist
lawyer
math
mechanic
nurse
office
office work
overtime
pay
pension plan
police officer
pressure
public speaking
qualities
responsibility
salary
satisfaction
skills
strengths
stress
taxi driver

teacher
teaching
team
traveling salesperson
typing
vacation
variety
vice president
warning
weekend

Verbs
affect
apply
be good at
be stuck
cope
correct
earn
exchange
graduate
manage
meet
organize
produce
quit
react
relax
swim
type
use
used to
wish

Modal verb
must

Adjectives
boring
challenging
dangerous
effective
exciting
free
good
interesting
personal
special
terrible
well
well-paid
worst

Adverbs
a little
at all
at times
less
more
OK
pretty
very

Other words
actually
long hours

Expressions
Sound great!
We'll be in touch.

Unit 3 Destinations

Grammar

1. Words commonly used as countable nouns

accident	computer	garden	lake	shower
address	country	group	library	storm
answer	crowd	handle	meeting	stream
apartment	daughter	head	message	street
bank	day	hill	mistake	suburb
beach	driver	hospital	month	teacher
bridge	effect	hotel	newspaper	thought
car	factory	house	picture	tourist
chapter	farm	idea	place	vacation
child	field	industry	problem	week
city	film	journey	program	year
college	friend	kitchen	room	

2. Words commonly used as uncountable nouns

agriculture	earth	freedom	marriage	safety
atmosphere	education	ground	nature	sightseeing
behavior	electricity	health	peace	technology
childhood	environment	history	pleasure	transportation
climate	experience	independence	pollution	travel
confidence	employment	industry	population	waste
courage	fashion	labor	poverty	weather
democracy	food			

Key Vocabulary

Nouns
American Indian
  (Native American)
artist
beach
center
city
climate
cost of living
country
crime
crowds
culture
drought
employment
flight
flood
hail
hometown
hostel
hotel
housing
humidity
industry
island
lightning
location
north
painter
park
place
pollution
population

poverty
public housing
resort
safety
shop
shopping
shower
sightseeing
size
snow
south
spring
storm
suburb
summer
sun
thunder
thunderstorm
tornado
tourist
tourist attraction
town
traffic
transportation
typhoon
unemployment
weather
wind
winter
year

Verbs
decide
like
live
visit

Modal verb
might

Adjectives
American
beautiful
Canadian
charming
cheap
delightful
excellent
famous
fantastic
farming
fascinating
fashionable
French-speaking
great
industrial
Italian
local
lovely
medieval
medium-sized
quiet
safe
seaside

southeast
tropical

Adverbs
about
far away
sometime
somewhere
unfortunately

Quantifiers
a few
a lot of
a little
enough
few
hardly any
lots of
no
not enough
not many
not much
plenty
plenty of
too many
too much

Other word
whereabouts

Expressions
It sounds like . . .
Sounds good!

Unit 4 What a story!

Grammar

Past tenses

> **Past tense**
> It **rained** all day.
> She **laughed.**
>
> **Past continuous**
> It **was raining** all day.
> She **was laughing.**
>
> **Past perfect**
> It **had rained** all day.
> She **had laughed.**
>
> **Past perfect continuous**
> It **had been raining** all day.
> She **had been laughing.**

Key Vocabulary

Nouns
actor
ambulance
building site
bus
case
cash
cat
chimney
church
coin
creature
cruise
dinner
dream
elevator
emergency landing
face
factory worker
flour mill
freeway
hand
headline
honeymoon
jewelry
key
magazine
man
mansion
money
neighbor
news
newspaper
noise
owner
passenger
pillow
plane
police
prime minister

radio
ring
road
robber
roof
store
suitcase
thief
TV (television)
UFO (unidentified
   flying object)
wedding
yacht

Verbs
admit
arrest
be involved in
borrow
break into
catch
claim
climb
come in
deny
drive
enter
fall asleep
feel
find
get
get out
get someone out of
get stuck
happen
hear
hide
land
lend
lick

move
put out
receive
release
return
rob
run away
see
send
sit
stand
steal
stop
subscribe
succeed
touch
try
uncover
wake up
walk
wear

Adjectives
angry
bizarre
born
drunk
injured
horrible
next
private
strange
stuck
wet
working-class

Adverbs
a few years ago
after
as
at night
daily
last night
last week
nearer
once
one time
recently
this morning
upside-down

Expression
What was it about?

Unit 5 Could you do me a favor?

Key Vocabulary

Nouns
afternoon
airport
camera
cassette player
letter
message
number
party
pencil
request
tapes
telephone
typewriter
Walkman

Verbs
be able to
bring
decline
give
go
help
let
mail
say
start
tell

Modal verbs
can
could
shall
should
will
would

Adjectives
brave
common
desperate
drunken
excited
fine
loud
nervous
quick
romantic
slow
soft
sorry
unusual

Adverbs
midnight
right now

Expressions
I wonder if you'd mind . . . ?
Would you mind if . . . ?
Would it be OK if . . . ?
Would you like to leave a message?

Go ahead.
By the way, . . .

Unit 6 Comparatively speaking

Key Vocabulary

Nouns
adult
air
arts and crafts
bank
botany
ceramics
clothes
community college
credit card
daytime
department store
designer label
dinner
dorms
dressmaking
education system
employee
evening
exam
foreign language
furniture
game
gift
government

hobby
humanities
jazz
kid
kindergarten
literature
loan
lunch
marriage
movie
music
novel
philosophy
physics
pop
preschool
price tag
private tutor
sciences
secondary school
specialty store
train
travel
uniform
university

Verbs
buy
choose
consider
fix up
learn
major in
mention
pay
prefer
read
replace
save
sell
study
take out
think
throw away
want

Adjectives
busy
carefree
cheaper
disciplined
domestic
easier
expensive
foreign
full-time
fun
hectic
junior
large
married
modern
necessary
organized
public
relaxing
self-employed
senior
separate
similar
single
small

Adverbs
rather
till
until

Quantifiers
all
both . . . and
many
most
neither . . . nor
none
not all
not many
some

Unit 7 Don't drink the water!

Key Vocabulary

Nouns
advantage
baby
bill
birthday
bottle of wine
Carnival
castle
cathedral
coast
countryside
customs
dormitory
fact
fall
flowers
hospital
mosque
museum
picture
prices
scenery
scholarship
river trip
temple
tip

Verbs
arrive
ask
bring along
enroll
get engaged
go out
invite
share
stay
take

Adjectives
all right
difficult
easy
extra
friendly
high
main
OK
poor
reasonable

Adverbs
abroad
more and more
next year
nowadays
on time
these days

Conjunctions
for
if
so
when

Other words
on business

Expressions
That sounds interesting!

Well, that depends . . .
One thing to remember is . . .

Unit 8 Getting things done

Key Vocabulary

Nouns
airplane
amusement park
architecture
area
birthday card
block
blood pressure
coffee
color
corner
date
day trip
door
dress
electronics store
eggs
fax
film
frozen food
grocery shopping
haircut
handicrafts
heel
hiking
history
live music
machine
meal
medical advice
milk
musician
passport
phone call
photo
photocopy
photocopy center
post office
repair shop
restroom
sales technique
shoe
shopping mall
snack
stamps
stereo
street
street vendor
suit
supermarket
theater
train station
visitor
watch

Verbs
check
deliver
develop
recommend
repair
service
shine

Adjectives
close
crowded
hard
popular
terrific

Adverbs
after class
around here
downtown
out-of-town
probably
weekdays

Expressions
Let me think.
It isn't running right.

Unit 9 Is that a fact?

Grammar

The future

> **With present simple**
> The manager **leaves** on Monday.
>
> **With present continuous**
> The manager **is leaving** on Monday.
>
> **With *going to***
> The manager **is going to leave** on Monday.
>
> **With *will***
> The manager **will leave** on Monday.
>
> **With future continuous**
> The manager **will be leaving** on Monday.
>
> **With future perfect**
> The manager **will have left** on Monday.

Key Vocabulary

Nouns
actress
aging
article
astronaut
author
behavior
biographer
biography
biology
business
cartoon movie
CD (compact disc)
century
chemistry
common cold
composer
cure
economist
emperor
engineer
event
explorer
future
grandmother
great-great-grandmother
human
independence
influence
inventor
jumbo jet
landmark
life
magnetic compass
management
market
mind
minerals
moon

mother
motorist
movie director
nationality
ocean
outer space
politician
population
president
product
psychologist
queen
quiz
researcher
revolution
robot
science
scientist
settlement
slavery
space
spacecraft
statue
surgeon
symphony
technology
trade
woman

Verbs
abolish
ban
become
build
change
clean
come down
compose
discover
gain
help
imagine
need
rule
run
sink

Adjectives
common
famous
first
medical
national
permanent
powerful
real
scary
solar-powered
typical
warm

Adverbs
about
since
till
within

Other words
in existence
in order to
supposed to

Unit 10 There's no place like home

Grammar

Adverbial clauses

Time
When I lived here, the neighborhood was pretty quiet.
Since she moved away, I haven't heard from her.

Condition
If if rains, we'll stay home.
Unless the weather improves, we'll stay home.

Purpose
They pulled down the building **in order to make a parking lot.**
They put up a fence **to keep out the neighbor's dog.**

Reason
We didn't like living there **because it was too noisy.**
Since the house was close to the road, it was very noisy.

Opposition
Although I enjoy reading, I don't read much these days.
Even though the hotel was expensive, we enjoyed staying there.

Key Vocabulary

Nouns
air conditioner
apartment building
appliance
balcony
bedroom
building
bulb
burner
cassette tape
central heating
color control
dial tone
fan
faucet
garden
hair dryer
handle
household chore
iron
kitchen
lamp
lens
light bulb
neighborhood
oven
patio
pool
portable color television
refrigerator
scratch
shopping center
stove
subway system
taxi
telephone
television

temperature control
view
window
yard

Verbs
burn
check on
come by
come over
cool
damage
fix
freeze
heat
look at
play

Adjectives
black and white
clear
cold
hot
older

Adverbs
also
as well (as)
away
besides
downstairs
in addition to
nearby
properly
right
right away
too

Conjunctions
also
although
even though
however

Expressions
What can I do for you?
What seems to be the matter?

126

Unit 11 What a world we live in!

Grammar

IF-clauses

Describing common occurrences
If I get a phone call when I'm in bed, I never answer it.

Describing common occurrences in the past
If the teacher asked me a question, I would always try to answer it.
If my mother was feeling tired, I usually prepared the meal.

Possible situations in the present
If you don't want to watch the TV, please turn it off.

Possible situations in the future
If I get a scholarship, I will go to college next year.

Unlikely situations
If I got an A on the test, I would be surprised.

Things that might have happened in the past but didn't
If I had studied harder, I would have passed the test.

Key Vocabulary

Nouns
acids
air pollution
bed
beer
can
carpet
chemicals
chinaware
cigarette advertising
company
corruption
cups
drugs
Earth
education
financial reward
first-class ticket
flexible hours
garbage disposal
health
high school graduate
inflation
jail
leader
medical costs
national holiday
outer space
plastic container
plates
pollution
private schools
public transportation
reason
soda
source
speed limit
test scores
tires
traffic noise
vacation
vandalism
vegetables

Verbs
agree
allow
buy
control
disagree
eliminate
face
handle
lay off (someone)
lower
make money
move in
provide
reduce
spend

Adjective
urgent

Other words
a three-day week
a trip around the world

Expressions
Gee, that's too bad!
That's a good point.
Yes, I agree with you.
That's true, but . . .
Maybe you're right, but . . .
Well, I disagree because . . .

127

Unit 12 How does it work?

Key Vocabulary

Nouns
back
bonsai tree
bottle
box
branch
broom
bucket
calculator
chips
compartment
container
corkscrew
cover
crossword puzzle
dishes
end
envelope
fertilizer
floppy disk
floor
function
gadget
glue
guarantee
hammer
instrument
leather
leaves

liquid
mailbox
microwave oven
model
ounce
paper mill
part
piggy bank
point
porcelain
pot
pulp
roots
saw
shape
sheet of paper
soil
steel
steel roller
string
stuff
switch
tea
teapot
temperature
toaster
tool
use
utensil

vacuum cleaner
wax
wire
wok
wood

Verbs
add
boil
carry
consist of
cook
cut
cut back
describe
dry
fit
flatten
grow
heat
hold
mix
open
pass
place
plant
polish
press
remove

stick together
sweep
tie
trim

Adjectives
curved
healthy
heavy
latest
pocket-size
portable
simple
thick
tiny
useless

Adverb
almost

Expressions
I have no idea.
How about this one?

Unit 13 That's a possibility

Grammar

Past modals

Impossibility
I **could not have left** my bag on the bus.

Expectation
She **should have arrived** by now.
She **ought to have arrived** by now.

Assumption/Certainty
Someone **must have come** here earlier.

Uncertainty
They **could have lost** their way.
She **might have forgotten** the telephone number.
He **may have overslept.**

Negative possibility
They **may not have known** about it.

Undesirable actions
He **shouldn't have stayed** so late.

Hypothetical situations
I **would not have done** that.

Key Vocabulary

Nouns
alien
ancient times
communication
compass
dinner party
dinosaur
first-aid kit
food concentrate
fun
gallon
heating unit
hunter
idea
invader
life raft
locksmith
matches
mystery
nylon rope
oxygen

parachute silk
place of worship
pyramid
radio
sailor
signal flare
solar-powered receiver-transmitter
spaceship
star
tank
theory
tow truck

Verbs
apologize
destroy
disappear
doubt
forget
guess
joke

keep out
kill off
prevent
refuse
remember
remind
run out of
serve
state
tease
turn up

Adjectives
considerate
cool
dehydrated
earlier
inconsiderate
unsolved

Adverb
in public

Expressions
That sounds crazy to me!
No one knows for sure.

Unit 14 The right stuff

Grammar

Adjectives ending in **-ing**

amazing	confusing	disturbing	interesting	relaxing
annoying	convincing	embarrassing	intimidating	rewarding
appalling	depressing	exciting	intriguing	satisfying
boring	disappointing	fascinating	outstanding	shocking
challenging	disgusting	frightening	pleasing	surprising
charming	distressing	infuriating	refreshing	terrifying

Key Vocabulary

Nouns
advertisement
advertising
batteries
bicycle
businessperson
camera work
chef
clothes
concept
design
electric outlet
frame
imagination
impression
job interview
jogging
language school
laptop computer
layout
photograph
running shoes
salesperson
slogan

TV commercial
TV program

Verbs
dress
fold
run a business
spend time
throw a party
weigh

Adjectives
aluminum
available
clever
comfortable
creative
dynamic
entertaining
friendly
hardworking
independent
informative
intelligent

light
lightweight
patient
practical
successful
tough
useful
well written

Adverbs
on sale
at 50% off

Expression
It really caught my eye!

129

Unit 15 It's a matter of opinion

Key Vocabulary

Nouns
army
breathing
cigarette
citizen
companies
day care
developing countries
driver
fail
fault
gambling
government official
harm
health care
law
lyrics
non-smoker
nuclear power plant
office worker
parking
pass
personal stereo
reason
restrictions
ride
rights
rock album
sales tax
tourism
violence
warning label

Verbs
advise
charge
congratulate
contradict
criticize
delay
deny
get sick of
grade
light up
package
point out
praise
propose

Adjectives
courteous
illegal
opposite
smokeless
strange
voluntary

Adverbs
anymore
anywhere
someday
wherever

Expressions
It's a matter of opinion.
Why do you say that?
I don't see it that way at all.
I'll have to think about it.
That's a good point.

Are you kidding?
Come on!

Irregular Verbs

Present	Past	Past Participle	Present	Past	Past Participle
be: am/is, are	was, were	been	lose	lost	lost
become	became	become	make	made	made
blow	blew	blown	meet	met	met
break	broke	broken	pay	paid	paid
bring	brought	brought	put	put	put
build	built	built	quit	quit	quit
burn	burned	burned	read	read	read
buy	bought	bought	run	ran	run
catch	caught	caught	say	said	said
choose	chose	chosen	see	saw	seen
come	came	come	sell	sold	sold
cut	cut	cut	send	sent	sent
dream	dreamed/dreamt	dreamed/dreamt	shine	shined/shone	shined/shone
drive	drove	driven	show	showed	shown
fall	fell	fallen	sink	sank	sunk
feel	felt	felt	sit	sat	sat
find	found	found	speak	spoke	spoken
forget	forgot	forgotten	spend	spent	spent
freeze	froze	frozen	stand	stood	stood
get	got	gotten	steal	stole	stolen
give	gave	given	stick	stuck	stuck
go	went	gone	sweep	swept	swept
grow	grew	grown	swim	swam	swum
hear	heard	heard	take	took	taken
hide	hid	hidden	teach	taught	taught
hold	held	held	tell	told	told
keep	kept	kept	think	thought	thought
lay	laid	laid	throw	threw	thrown
leave	left	left	wake	woke	woken
let	let	let	wear	wore	worn
light	lit	lit	write	wrote	written

Active and Passive Verbs

Tense	Active	Passive
Present simple	She drives it.	It is driven.
Present continuous	She is driving it.	It is being driven.
Present perfect	She has driven it.	It has been driven.
Present perfect continuous	She has been driving it.	It has been being driven.*
Past simple	She drove it.	It was driven.
Past continuous	She was driving it.	It was being driven.
Past perfect	She had driven it.	It had been driven.
Past perfect continuous	She had been driving it.	It had been being driven.*
Future	She will drive it.	It will be driven.
Future continuous	She will be driving it.	It will be being driven.
Future perfect	She will have driven it.	It will have been driven.
Future perfect continuous	She will have been driving it.	It will have been being driven.*

*The perfect continuous tenses are not used very often in the passive voice.

Answers to Unit 7, Exercise 13

Here is how an American or Canadian would usually respond to the culture check:

1 Y (women greeting men or other women; men greeting women)
2 Y
3 Y
4 N (but OK among friends)
5 N
6 N
7 N
8 N (not common in apartment buildings in large cities, but often common in small towns and neighborhoods)
9 Y
10 N
11 N
12 Y (North Americans don't like people to arrive early, but don't usually mind if guests arrive a little late)
13 N (however, this may be OK in small towns)
14 Y
15 Y
16 N (it's polite to call first and ask if it's OK)
17 Y (if there's plenty of food)
18 Y (but friends often take turns paying for the whole check when they go out together regularly)
19 N
20 Y
21 N
22 N

Answers to Review of Units 7–9, Exercise 4.1

a) There are too many to make a complete list, but here are a few: The Bee Gees, The Eagles, Fleetwood Mac, The Rolling Stones, Simon and Garfunkel.
b) Albert Einstein
c) In 1947
d) John Fitzgerald Kennedy, U.S. President (1961–1963)
e) He was the founder of psychoanalysis.

Answers to Unit 14, Exercise 9

"Designed to be seen and not heard": Hewlett-Packard personal computer printers
"Quality is Job 1": Ford Motor Company cars
"Don't leave home without it": American Express cards
"We cover the four corners of the Earth": The International Publications of Time Inc. magazines
"Because your signature deserves the best": Parker fountain pens

Answers to Unit 14, Exercise 10

Answers to Unit 12, Exercise 2

#1 sewing machine = It's a machine that's used for stitching material together. It's made of metal or plastic and has a needle. It's run by hand or by electricity.

#2 shoehorn = It's an object that's usually made of metal or plastic. It's used to help get your feet into shoes.

Answer to Unit 14, Exercise 8

Sanyo "IntelliTuner" car radio

Answers to Interchange 13

_15_ box of matches

_4_ food concentrate

_6_ 50 feet of nylon rope

_8_ parachute silk

_13_ portable heating unit

_11_ two pistols

_12_ one case of dehydrated milk

_1_ two 100-pound tanks of oxygen

_3_ map of the stars as seen from the moon

_9_ life raft

_14_ magnetic compass

_2_ five gallons of water

_10_ signal flares

_7_ first-aid kit

_5_ solar-powered receiver-transmitter

(From the National Aeronautics and Space Administration)